Trust and faith
beautifully wove

From a childhood with a blind parent to extended sexual
abuse to two miscarriages to numerous major surgeries to
a devastating cancer diagnosis, Shireen's journey has been
daunting. Yet even as the fabric of her life has revealed
varying hues, because of her deep trust in God, Shireen
has consistently leaned into His faithfulness. Wrap
yourself in her story… soak in her lessons of comfort and
provision… and embrace the God who loves us through
all of the colours of our lives.

—Ann Mainse
Heart to Heart Marriage & Family Ministries
Author, Speaker, TV Host of *A Better Us*

In *Big Challenges, Even Bigger God*, Shireen shares her
story with transparency and explores every moment in
which she faced overwhelming trials. Her determination
to walk through fires with faith is deeply inspiring. God's
fingerprints and the evidence of His presence in these
moments are explicit. How great is our God that He can
reach His hands down from heaven to carry us through
moments that seem insurmountable. Thank you,
Shireen, for the courage you had to write this memoir
that points back to our Heavenly Father and His deep
resounding love.

—Cyndi Desjardins Wilkens
International Speaker
Author of *Shine On: The Remarkable True Story
of a Quadruple Amputee*

Big Challenges, Even Bigger God presents a glimpse into the real life and real faith of a wife, mother, and pastor. Shireen Spencer passionately and brilliantly epitomizes the truth that life does not have to be perfect to be fulfilling, whilst navigating the experiences of life. This book is more than just a great read—it's a road map for successful living in the face of adversity.

—Richard J. Brown
Lead Pastor, Kingsway Community Life Centre
Toronto, ON

This book will inspire you! The stories regarding Shireen's life will help you to see a big God who truly works in the good and bad experiences in your life for something good. A positive and godly perspective on life's problems. If you are currently going through a life storm, this book will encourage you to keep trusting God, no matter what situation you are facing.

—Rev. Dr. Tina Pitamber, B.Sc., M.Div., D.Min.
Lead Pastor, Solid Rock Community Church of the Nazarene
Richmond Hill, ON

Big Challenges, Even Bigger GOD

*Finding God
Faithful in the Hard
Moments of Life*

Shireen Spencer

Printed in Canada

ISBN: 978-1-4866-1805-7

Word Alive Press
119 De Baets Street Winnipeg, MB R2J 3R9
www.wordalivepress.ca

Cataloguing in Publication information can be obtained from Library and Archives Canada.

ACKNOWLEDGEMENTS

I wrote lyrics to a song many years ago. It truly speaks to how I feel God is working in my life.

And my life is a song written by the Holy One.
Each lyric penned with purpose and with pride.
For each day that I live, I'll be careful to give praise
To the One who writes the story of my life.[1]

I owe my story, and how it is being used, to God my Saviour. He has given me beauty for ashes many times during my life. I am grateful to Him. I thank God for His love and patience, and for His mercy and grace. I am humbled that He has given purpose to my life. I am nothing without Him.

I am thankful to my parents. The godly heritage and legacy that they have passed on to me has shaped and filled my life. Mom and Dad, I am who I am because of the example both of you have set for me.

I am beyond blessed that God has given me a supportive husband who has always believed in me and encouraged me to be and do my best. Che, you and your love are a big part of my story! I look forward to the chapters God is still writing. I couldn't do this without you! Thank you for your prayers. They mean the world to me. Thank you to my boys who think Mommy can do anything! You keep me dreaming and achieving.

There have been so many friends and prayer partners who spoke this book into existence years before I even penned it. I am thankful for these supportive, godly women who believed in me when I didn't believe in myself—Vanessa, Mona, Kim, Trudy, Tina, Leanne, Aisha, and Cyndi. Thank you for helping me find my voice in this way. There are not enough words to express my gratitude.

Thank you to Ann Mainse, who listened to part of my story the first time we met and prayed for me and spoke a word into my future. The seed you planted took root, and the journey started because of you.

Thank you to Cyndi Desjardins Wilkens, who is an inspiration and encouragement to my ministry and life. You are a true cheerleader to me in this new journey.

To Renae Jarrett, my new friend, coach, and editor, whom God brought into my life for such a time as this! Thank you for your support, prayers, and gentle way of helping me accept how God has gifted me.

INTRODUCTION

There have been so many people—friends and acquaintances, even strangers—who have told me that I need to share my story. I had never thought that my personal experiences and life events were so drastic or amazing that they required sharing in this way, but I realize now that my story doesn't have to be a great tragedy to show the faithfulness of God. Most people just want to know how to live through their everyday, normal struggles. There will always be someone going through something much more difficult than I have experienced, but if there are moments in my journey that can help anyone, I am willing to tell the whole story. We all have something to overcome in some way, at some time. This is my story of being an ongoing overcomer.

I try to be a happy person. I am pretty optimistic about life, and truly enjoy laughing and staying positive. For me, it isn't a facade. I don't even really do it to make others happy. I choose joy because that is what I want. It is the only way I know how to rise above circumstances and truly be able to live the verse, *"...the joy of the Lord is your strength"* (Nehemiah 8:10).

What I have learned on my journey is that life is indeed that—a daily journey. Finding God at work in my life has been a journey of daily choices. It's true that I have to want to hear from God to actually hear from God. I have to take the time to listen to Him, and to open my eyes to look and see what He is doing. I have to expect to receive from Him to actually receive from Him. I have to choose to be in His presence to receive His presence. I have to search for Him to find Him.

The Word of God has always been an essential part of my life, as I grew up with my parents modelling that there was no way to live without it. God has spoken to me through Scripture. I have held on tightly to the Word of God and have found it to be true. Memorizing Scripture, so that it is part of my daily vocabulary and prayer life, has helped me tremendously in hearing from God and being given just what I need at the moments when I need it. It really is my daily bread. There are days when it feels like the words of Scripture are a love letter written to me personally at just the right time. I approach reading my Bible with the expectation that it will have a message just for me, at just the right time, to give guidance or healing or strength or whatever I need.

The lyrics from worship songs are like words coming right from the mouth of God to my ears and heart at just the right time, too. When I turn on the music in the car or my home and just let harmonies and melodies fill the space I'm in, it's amazing how sweet, intimate and clear the message of God can be to me. I couldn't do without my music. God touches my heart in such a deep way through praise and worship.

Prayer time is like oxygen to me. I do pray without ceasing. God and I are always in communication. Sometimes I talk too much, but I am learning to be a better listener. This is something that takes a lifetime of practice! I have also learned to sit in silence with my thoughts and my feelings, offering to God every part of me. He receives it and just allows me to feel His presence. I have surrounded myself with committed, consistent prayer partners—I don't know what I would do without these cherished friends who pray for me daily or monthly. I am beyond thankful. I hear the heart of God through prayers and messages from dear friends and pastors. My own life is encouraged, and I get excited to pray for others and watch God answer. He is continually speaking.

God uses everything to get my attention. Even the beauty of the earth and its changing seasons are messages from God to my heart. Nature speaks so loudly to me. My various life experiences also tell me secrets I might have missed if I hadn't gone through them. I haven't always enjoyed everything that God has made part of my journey, but I would never give up the closeness with God that I have been blessed with because I chose to go through these experiences with Him.

To hear God speak with different expressions and passion, I need to be fed through His Word and worship. I need to surround myself with good friendships and a praying church. I need to serve others—to be sure that I am being used by Him to be a blessing to someone else. All of these tools and practices are like bread and water to me. They have fed me and helped me to keep going; to walk the journey and never give up! May that same determination be yours as you read this book.

Chapter One
PRACTICE MAKES POWER

Life hasn't been easy for me. Although my life hasn't been bad, neither has it been without great struggle! Most of my life has been hard. Where do I begin? Do I tell you about being a sickly child, always having too many infections or allergic reactions, and giving my parents frequent scares? Do I tell you about my father going blind from glaucoma, and the changes that this brought to my family? Do I tell you about the sexual abuse I experienced at the hands of a man who served in the church? Do I tell you about getting a scholarship to university and losing it because of my deteriorating mental state? Do I tell you about my own struggle with glaucoma and then asthma? Maybe you want to hear about my many car accidents, the first happening right after I'd received my first contract with a school board and just months before my first teaching assignment. Do I tell you about the year I was terribly sick, seeing so many doctors and specialists with so many pending surgeries that the operating room became a constant? Do I tell you about the vocal nodules that prevented me from being able to sing or speak for a year? I am sure that you can identify with my many financial struggles and unsuccessful attempts to complete something I'd started. I have been there more times than I'd like! Perhaps you want to hear about the fibroids and empty womb, or the two miscarriages?

I could begin with the last three years of my life, which spiralled from bad to worse—being told that I needed to go into surgery without knowing what they were going to find, and then at the same time being wrongly accused of physical misconduct as a teacher, not to mention the six surgeries and complications that followed! How about my battle with cancer? There have been too many challenging experiences in my physical reality to go into detail or even list them all, but what I've learned is that for each struggle, God has revealed Himself in ways that have brought growth to my life. Most importantly, these struggles have brought me closer to knowing this God Whom I love.

I want to begin by telling you about the faithfulness of God in my life in spite of all I have listed. I prefer to begin there because it truly is by the grace of God that I am where I am today. That is the message I want you to hear through every story I tell. God is and will always be faithful.

Some people may believe that these are just words or "Christianese," but to me, they are true words that I live by. I truly am alive today—not struggle-free, but enjoying life because of what God has done for me. I wish I could explain it better. I wish there was more to say, but there just isn't. It really is as simple as that for me! I have taken God at His Word and held on to His Word, because that is what has been modelled for me. It has been passed on to me to keep trusting God and going to Him, and I made the choice to believe that this was the only way for me to live.

My father went blind when I was about ten years old, and that became our new normal. Life was all about navigating my father's blindness—in my heart, in my thoughts, and in my physical reality. I am sure it was a drastic change for my parents.

It has been thirty-five years since then, and what remains in my memory about that time is the importance of prayer. Prayer is still my first response for every situation I face.

My parents have always been people of prayer. My childhood memories are filled with moments from prayer meetings. I remember late-night prayer meetings, all-night prayer meetings, house prayer meetings, church prayer meetings. As much as my young self was annoyed at constantly being dragged to such events or always having them in our home, they shaped me and my perspective or schema on life.

Prayer was the way my parents fought their continual life battles, whether related to glaucoma or other problems. It's a pretty good battle plan, I would say. My parents' life motto has been a mix of "Pray without ceasing," "In everything give thanks, for this is God's will," and "Make your supplication unto God with thanksgiving." So these Scriptures and this attitude have taught me to embrace the difficult chapters of my life, too.

I have learned that there is no prayer that God can't handle. I have come to Him screaming in anger, crying in hurt, laughing in disbelief, or without much to say at all. I have come to Him in doubt or in fear. I have come to Him just because that was what I wanted to do. He is my friend. I have learned persistence. I have learned that God answers in His own time and in His own way, but He does answer. I have learned that prayer isn't really about the answer I want, but about the answer I need—and about the One who gives the answer. I am to pray when things make sense, and when they don't. I am to

> I have learned that prayer isn't really about the answer I want, but about the answer I need—and about the One who gives the answer.

believe until there is no breath left in me. I am to pray and praise always. I am to read and receive His Word, even through tears!

Confession time: I don't know everything, so I have to choose to trust the One who does!

> *Trust in the Lord with all your heart, And lean not on your own understanding; In all your ways acknowledge Him, and He shall direct your paths.* (Proverbs 3:5–6)

I have certainly learned that God and I don't think alike. But He did tell me ahead of time that this would be the case!

> *"For my thoughts are not your thoughts, neither are your ways my ways," declares the Lord.* (Isaiah 55:8, NIV)

Life isn't without battles and hardships. But even when I've thought that I couldn't take anymore or go any further, I have been able to look back and see that His grace has truly been enough. I don't know how, and sometimes I may not have thought I felt His strength, but I'm still here! I'm still going forward.

Confession time again: I take God at His word, even if something He has promised doesn't appear like it is happening. Call me naive, but I trust Him to make sense of it all. As you read through my stories, you may not feel like God has always answered my prayers. To be honest with you, sometimes I don't either, but I *know* He has, with His presence and with His best for me. He is for me and is working everything out for His good. I have already been told ahead of time that in this world I will have many troubles, but I can be of good cheer because He has overcome the world—and He can help me do the same.

Chapter Two
MONEY DOESN'T GROW ON TREES

No, money doesn't grow on trees—but God always brings fruit!
What stands out about my childhood is how faithful God was to
provide. We always had the clothes we needed, and more often
than not, our wants were covered too. This might not seem like
much, but to children, fashion and style matter! We did a lot of
shopping trips with my parents. I remember the pretty dresses
and perfect shoes. I always felt like a princess. There was always
food on the table. It may not have been a lot or even what we
liked, but we could never say we were starved!

I have fond memories of youth group outings, summer camp
experiences, visits to the U.S. for family, missions trips and more.
I had a pretty normal and fulfilling childhood. My parents taught
us that God always provided, and we lived and held on to the
truth we found in Scriptures.

*And my God shall supply all your needs according to His
riches in glory by Christ Jesus.* (Philippians 4:19)

He shall be like a tree
Planted by the rivers of water,
That brings forth its fruit in its season,
Whose leaf also shall not wither;
And whatever he does shall prosper. (Psalm 1:3)

For he shall be like a tree planted by the waters,
Which spreads out its roots by the river,
And will not fear when heat comes;
But its leaf will be green,
And will not be anxious in the year of drought,
Nor will cease from yielding fruit. (Jeremiah 17:8)

God continually brought practical and spiritual fruit into our lives, yet my family never had a lot of money. Sometimes we struggled a lot. It must have been hard to raise a family of four children on basically one salary for most of our lives, yet my parents were generous to a fault. I'm sure there were many financial hardships I didn't know about as a child. There was more month than money many times, and bad financial choices mixed with generosity. The ones I knew of were more than enough! There were times we didn't know how a bill was going to be paid or groceries bought. I remember the many times we didn't have a car or even money for the transit, and church families took the time, making more than one trip to bring our family back and forth.

We were very blessed. Financial hardships were great, but God's provision was even greater. I have held on tightly to the Word of God and have found it to be true. Through it all, we prayed and praised as a family. We cried lots. We read and received the Word. We found God to be faithful and to be our Provider.

Chapter Three

SOMETHING OUT OF NOTHING

I don't like winter, although I love freshly fallen snow. I can enjoy the beauty of it as long as I am inside. I remember one ski trip we took as a family—my husband Che loves to ski. Up at the chalet, I walked around with a good friend and enjoyed the scenery. I also did what I loved to do: I shopped, and then returned to the condo to prepare meals for the hungry men who would be coming back from the slopes. I didn't mind the cold this time. The warmth of the sun on my face and my baby enjoying crunching in the snow were the things that memories are made of, although our firstborn was unfortunately too young to remember the good time he'd had here. This was a much-needed trip that came as a surprise and a gift. I love surprises, especially when they come from God. I don't even think I properly thanked the person God used to bless us with the trip, but I thank God over and over again for it now.

No matter the season, God was faithful to us. I remember another time when the boys splashed around, so giddy over being able to run from our room right down the hill into the lake.

I closed my eyes tightly every time they did that, but secretly laughed loudly inside my heart at the amount of fun they were having. I can't swim, but they should have been born whales! They love the water. They went back and forth between the hotel pool and the lake outside. Their dad was busy that summer with them, but he wouldn't have had it any other way! We would never have gone to this place if not for the invitation. I didn't even know it existed! It was beautiful, and God was creating beautiful family memories. Our boys still speak about this vacation. God blessed us at just the right time… again.

The truths I learned as a child growing up with my parent's financial hardships followed me into my married life. There are so many times when God provided during my family's financial challenges. These memories shared above come from times when we didn't have the money. At both times, my heart was so broken that I thought the many pieces would never be put back together. But God gave me innumerable smiles to count on my boys' faces. He gave me photos to look back on, and I can now look at them and say that those were some of the best days of my life.

God continued to come through for us, and to be so faithful. He has given me many memories to be thankful for, and when the moments of life come where I am right in the midst of a struggle, I can look back and be reminded of those times or others—like when we were given an anonymous gift of $500

> Life is a mix of struggles and victories. It is never just one or the other, but an ebb and flow of both.

just when a bill was due for that amount, and we didn't know how we were going to pay it, or when a friend wrote a cheque for a large amount and told us to make sure that we spent it on Christmas gifts for our boys, or when another cheque came and we were instructed to use it on a vacation for our family. God continued to use the family of God at significant times in our lives to show us that He was in control! Dark seasons are a part of the rhythm of life.

Life is a mix of struggles and victories. It is never just one or the other, but an ebb and flow of both.

I will never be alone. God is with me, and has sent His love through human hands so many times. All these memories are treasures money can't buy… well, my money couldn't! God's accounting has created abundance in our lives. Through financially challenging times, I once again used the only proven formula that I know—Pray, Praise, Cry, and Read and Receive the Word. Repeat. I have learned that in God's economy there is only one currency, and that is blessing. It's not always financial, but so much more. It's provision for what we need. I have learned to always be grateful and count my blessings.

Philippians 4:13 says¸ *"I can do all things through Christ who strengthens me."*

I remember being ready for a new adventure. God had called me, and I was doing my Master's in Theology. I had taken time off teaching to devote a year to full-time study. I was excited about what I was learning, although I couldn't believe that I was a student again after having a break from studying and being in the workforce. I am more of an experiential learner and actually don't like being a student, but there was an excitement about obeying God that kept me in a place of anticipation. I had saved up what I needed, and was so thankful to the Lord that my needs were taken care of although I wasn't working. I made good friends and received great grades. After awhile, I went back to the classroom while studying at night. It isn't usual protocol to be a permanent teacher on leave and also get on the supply teacher list, but one door opened after another with great ease, as if it was just waiting tailor-made for me. I was loving the adventure of being in different schools, perhaps because I got to choose the ones I went to, and at each one there were friends of mine who were teachers and principals. I was favoured. I got work daily and ended up doing a full-time, long-term position. I had it made! This was certainly the hand of God, and it left me no choice but to be thankful.

> *Rejoice always, pray without ceasing, in everything give thanks; for this is the will of God in Christ Jesus for you.* (1 Thessalonians 5:16–18)

I had it made! Now, when you hear that statement and read about the events I just described, you would think life was going well. Not so! It was again difficult—challenging. Totally not what I had planned. It wasn't supposed to happen that way: I had no intention of going back to teaching so soon while doing my Master's in that year. Yet that was the situation I found myself in. I had to take a break from my study plan due to financial complications for my family.

I was upset. I was hurt. I was angry over how this situation had come about, and couldn't believe that God would allow me to be in this position. I had made good decisions and plans. I had obeyed God, but I was now suffering because of bad choices that weren't made by me. I had a choice to make. I could stay bitter or I could realize that God had made good things happen even in the midst of a difficult situation.

I prayed lots and let God know how I felt. I told God I didn't like this situation at all, but I loved Him and was going to trust Him. He answered by reminding me that He was working it all out. I was comforted, and kept following my trusted cycle. I prayed. I praised. I cried. I read and received the Word, and repeated this verse:

And we know that all things work together for good to those who love God, to those who are called according to His purpose. (Romans 8:28)

The finances I had saved, although not used the way I thought they would be, were a great help to my family. The money I thought I had given up to go on leave (since I couldn't go back and ask for my position) was replaced by full-time supply teaching. God once again provided in ways I could not have imagined! I completed that year in awe of how God had provided answers for my questions and dollars for my financial needs. I enjoyed the variety in life, although it was a hard year. Afterwards, I went back to teaching and gave studying a break, as I needed to regroup. I wasn't sure what God was doing, but I continued giving thanks and following His lead.

For I know the thoughts that I think toward you, says the Lord, thoughts of peace and not of evil, to give you a future and a hope. (Jeremiah 29:11)

However, I really wanted to finish what I had started, so a few years later I changed my program to better fit into my life and schedule. I changed to the modular program of the Master in Theological Studies. The people we started with weren't the ones we graduated with. It seemed like everyone in the class had big problems. It was so interesting how many in that program were in intense battles in their lives. One woman came from a different country and had a tragic story involving the breaking of her back. She was a busy mom to many children, but she felt led by God to finish her studies. She was pastoring a church plant voluntarily, and her financial needs were great. Another woman ended up being diagnosed with cancer and had to leave. I myself was having a terrible pregnancy, and then once my son was born my husband lost his job. The illness I was fighting then spiralled again. Yet again, I battled with how I was going to complete the year as circumstances tried to steal success from me in the area of health and finances.

This class prayed hard together for each other. Our professors prayed hard for us and with us. It was like no other school experience. Many times, many of us asked God what was going on, not just for ourselves but for the many needs we carried for our newly found friends.

"Lord, please fix this!"

"God, please provide."

"How long are we going to be stuck in this season?"

"Why did you bring me here to...?"

It was a class filled with needs, but it was also a class filled with ministry to one another. It was a class in which miracles happened. My struggles were put aside, and many times I felt they were irrelevant when I was praying for others. I went to class just to be able to help others. I always wanted to know from week to week what the praise reports were, or how much more we needed to press on in prayer.

It was a hard time for me, but it was hard for so many. Our class raised money for a student to feed her family for awhile. It was a timely surprise for her. We prayed for our friend with cancer just before her surgery. It went well. During my health struggles in this year, I was shown such great compassion from my professors. They showed great empathy and gave timely extensions. I persevered and overcame the challenges. The greatest miracle came when I thought I would have to miss another semester because we just couldn't afford it. Unbeknownst to me, there was a scholarship available for which a professor could recommend a student. I won that scholarship, and it paid for everything I needed at that time.

…being confident of this very thing, that He who has begun a good work in you will complete it until the day of Jesus Christ… (Philippians 1:6)

There were many more struggles to my Master's journey, but God continued to come through. He was really confirming in my heart and life that I was to serve God and serve others. If I kept my eyes on Him, He took care of the rest. Every time it seemed like I wouldn't have enough, I turned to God again. He not only provided, He showed up! In the midst of every struggle, God is there. I just have to confess that reality.

> If I kept my eyes on Him, He took care of the rest.

God is our refuge and strength,
A very present help in trouble. (Psalm 46:1)

I found God time and time again. He is so good. He always provided, and always will.

Chapter Four
BEAUTY FOR ASHES

It was the era of Michael W. Smith and Amy Grant. We sang a lot of their songs at the top of our lungs as we travelled on the buses for youth group or missions trips. We were those teens, sticking our heads out of the bus windows, singing, waving, and laughing in between the lyrics. We were silly and happy. Those were the good old days. I don't know how the more mature adults handled it! They must have really loved us.

One of those trips is forever etched in my memory. It was one of the last missions trips I did as a youth. How many young people get to go and make a difference in the lives of so many people—from babies to seniors? These lives were precious to the Lord, and I was so privileged to be a part of what God was doing.

The acoustics of the barn were second to none. Even those who couldn't sing sounded beautiful in the depth and space of this room as we gathered to praise God and pray for one another. These moments were precious, strengthening us for the challenges ahead of ministering to families in great need. They needed clothes and food. They needed medicine. They needed jobs. I wondered how my presence was helping them, and soon found out that they needed practical hands to show that someone cared. We enjoyed fellowship. I babysat the most beautiful baby girl with jewel blue, clear, ocean-coloured eyes. I cleaned. I took food to them. I served, and this made my heart very glad. They needed Jesus, and I was able to share His love and lead people to a relationship with Him. This was an experience I would never forget. This trip changed my life forever! I am still in awe of how God used me. He was working to strengthen and heal their lives.

Blessed be the God and Father of our Lord Jesus Christ, the Father of mercies and God of all comfort, who comforts us in all our tribulation, that we may be able to comfort those who are in any trouble, with the comfort with which we ourselves are comforted by God. (2 Corinthians 1:3–4)

Negatives only produce great photos in darkness. When they are finally done and exposed to the light, what they reveal is beautiful and can be enjoyed. God can take what was very painful and dark, and make beauty from ashes. He has done that for me. His light shines in through my dark spaces.

One of the most painful experiences in my life happened when I was just embarking on adulthood and doing what the Lord called me to do. I was sexually abused by a man in leadership at the church. It happened over a period of months, starting while I was volunteering at

> Negatives only produce great photos in darkness. When they are finally done and exposed to the light, what they reveal is beautiful and can be enjoyed. God can take what was very painful and dark, and make beauty from ashes.

the church I attended, continuing while I was leading a missions trip, and only ending when we returned home. There are many things about this time in my life I could have done differently. I could have told someone sooner. I could have positioned myself in such a way that it didn't happen again or multiple times. Who knows? Saying "would've, could've, should've" doesn't change the fact that it happened, or the heartache that took years to repair.

The night before our youth group left to go on the missions trip that I had looked forward to all year, my vision of what God was going to do in me and through me became a mess of confusion and questions! Since we were going to leave so early in the morning, it had been decided that we would all stay at the church and sleep there so that no one was late for the designated time when we would embark on this amazing adventure. It sure was an adventure, but not what I was expecting. It was amazingly hard and painful, but surprising in seeing what God can do with a mess. His strength is surely made perfect in my weakness. His grace is truly sufficient.

The boys slept downstairs and the girls upstairs. I have never been one to sleep well or comfortably outside of my own bed. Truth be told, I don't even sleep well there! When I can't sleep, I spend time in prayer or worship. It has always been a natural habit of mine. No one taught me this; I just figured I might as well do something valuable with my time. But through the years it has served me well, and I am so thankful to have continued growing in this discipline. I am sure it is what prevented that time from being even worse than what I experienced.

While we were all supposed to be sleeping, I heard my name called. It was a whisper, but an urgent one. I looked up and there he was at the door, calling me. I got out of bed and went to the office outside of the room we were in. I was the designated female leader for the trip, so I thought there was a problem that needed to be solved.

There certainly was a problem, but I could never have imagined what I was about to face. He pulled me onto his lap and reached to caress my breast, then planted a kiss on my lips. The room was spinning and the actions happened so fast, with no room for me to breathe. I couldn't get my thoughts to catch up to my reality. When I did, it had already happened. I ran out of the office and into the room of sleeping, young girls. The sight and sound of those girls should have been nothing less than peaceful, but for me it was the beginning of a very dark storm.

The morning came fast. The sun rose early and bright, but in my soul there was nothing but darkness. I had no time to even let the clouds show. I went on the trip anyway, because I couldn't let them down. How could I be responsible for ruining a missions trip? How could I prevent these lives from experiencing the mission of a lifetime that they had all worked so hard to go on? So I smiled, and went on as if nothing had happened. I couldn't let anyone know what happened the night before, so I made the choice to let it remain a secret. I just moved on with the day that everyone else was enjoying.

Later, "please don't" was all I could say, not knowing that I had already been violated again. I was standing in a communal wash-room in the barn that was to be our home for the week. There was one washroom for the males and one for the females. I thought I was safe because, being a very private person, I had chosen to get up early before anyone else would think of waking to go have a shower in private. I figured that I was safe because I was quiet, and I was the only one on the trip that was such an early bird. I was wrong. Maybe I wasn't so quiet in my movements, or perhaps he had outsmarted me by watching and waiting on my every move. I walked out of the shower with my towel on, only to be faced with the truth that I had shared this space unknowingly. He was waiting for me. He stretched out his hand to take off my towel and to let me know that he thought I was beautiful. What did he mean?

On our way to this location of ministry, we'd had to stop halfway. The trip would have been too long to do it in one day, so we broke it up, and were billeted in someone's home overnight. It was a beautiful home, and the host was warm and welcoming. The meals were delicious. I can still smell the waves of fresh baking rising into the atmosphere. I can hear the innocent laughter around the table as we listened to stories of what God had done in people's lives. The sound of loud snoring when I really wanted to sleep still makes me chuckle. Although I don't remember the names of everyone there, the faces of those beautiful people still remain with me.

But that memory is relived through shattered glass. The picture is no longer as beautiful as it could have been. I didn't know until that moment in the barn washroom that when he told me I was beautiful, it was because he had watched me undress, shower, and get dressed through the keyhole of that beautiful home's bathroom. How could all of this have happened without him being caught? How was it possible that no one saw what was happening to me?

Unbelievably, God was able to work through this pain, using me to be a blessing in the lives of the younger girls I was responsible for and also the families we ministered to while away. I told myself that I couldn't do anything about my pain and the situation that I was in, and that I wasn't about to waste this trip since we were so far from home. We worked with families and helped to repair broken-down homes in areas of great poverty. We took care of seniors in a great deal of pain who just needed someone to help clean and cook. We took care of babies while their moms tried to find work. Those people are forever etched in my memory. I know that Jesus' love was shown to them, and that one day I will see them again in heaven.

At that time in my life, that was my wish and my consolation. While there was darkness in my life, I was able to bring light to them. I remember wonderful times of praise and prayer happening, even while the enemy was at work against me. I took up my cross and followed Jesus into serving. Serving God and others takes your mind off yourself. Boy, did I need to think about something besides myself! I had every reason to be selfish, but I couldn't. Love was still compelling me forward—God's love. I was thankful that He was able to use me. The joy on the outside could only have been the Lord, because the sorrow inside was trying hard to pull me down. I kept my eyes on Jesus. I cried lots when no one was looking. I muffled my cries and dried my tears with my pillow. Prayer. Praise. Cry. Read and receive the Word. Repeat.

I held onto God, and let Him hold me. It was all I could do. I held onto the Scriptures, and those Scriptures are still the ones that carry me through different dark times in life. I believed that I was not alone, as I still believe now.

And the Lord, He is the One who goes before you. He will be with you, He will not leave you nor forsake you; do not fear nor be dismayed. (Deuteronomy 31:8)

Yet in all these things we are more than conquerors through Him who loved us. For I am persuaded that neither death nor life, nor angels nor principalities nor powers, nor things present nor things to come, nor height nor depth, nor any other created thing, shall be able to separate us from the love of God which is in Christ Jesus our Lord. (Romans 8:37–39)

The many truths in Psalm 139 carried me then and continue to carry me today!

Unfortunately, when we returned home this situation didn't come to an end. What I haven't told you yet is that the person who violated me was married. His wife had just had a baby. She and I were close—we had spent lots of time together in their home—and one day she invited me to stay overnight. I didn't want to say no. I didn't want things to change between us. I wanted things to stay normal.

Please—don't judge me. As a young person I valued my relationship with her, and didn't know how to avoid the situation while keeping our friendship intact.

I didn't think there was any way that he would be so bold as to try anything again, as we were in his home and his wife was present. If I just acted normally, everything would be fine. Right?

Wrong! The evening went well. I spent a wonderful time hanging out with his wife and playing with the baby. We cooked in the kitchen and enjoyed great conversation. My fears were only mine. They were not shared with or obvious to anyone else. I prayed a lot inside and laughed a lot outside.

However, the night came fast. I was tucked away in a bedroom in the basement while the family remained upstairs, far away from me—surely too far for any problem to come my way. But the enemy is able to sneak in and fit through the tiniest of spaces. He is able to turn something apparently safe into something so very dangerous. He makes opportunities out of things we wouldn't imagine. Yes, the night came and passed quickly, but it was the morning that surprised me! I awoke from a surprisingly comfortable sleep to the mouth-watering smell of well-cooked eggs and homemade biscuits. Remember: I don't sleep well, especially not in another bed, and even more so in the home of an abuser, but this night I had—at least for a few hours.

She must have been the one busy in the kitchen, distracted by cooking and the baby, because he came to get me. I heard the knock on the bedroom door and then it quickly opened. As fast as it had opened, it closed, leaving both of us on the same side of the door. The next thing I knew, we were both in the bed and my safe space changed. I guess the time wasn't too long or unusual, because we heard her sweet voice calling for breakfast. In my vague recollection, there was a response that just let her know he was coming up and I was getting ready. Although what had already taken place was bad, her voice stopped the worst from happening. I am so thankful for God's intervention! Psalm 139 became real to me again. There is no place where I am not in God's presence. He stretches out His hand and saves me.

You will be proud of me. After this incident, I cut ties from both of them. I was sad for her and me. He tried to beg me to continue being friends, promising that he would stop and that he had gone to God and repented.

If that's true, I am glad. God is a forgiving God. I needed to have God forgive and heal me, and he needed God's forgiveness too. But the process of forgiveness did not need to be done in each other's company.

To be violated and have any innocence stolen from you is a hard thing to work through. To go through it alone without anyone to share it with is even harder in some ways, I think. To finally share and be blamed is the hardest. That all happened to me. The enemy really does come to kill, steal and destroy, and he was trying to destroy me in every way.

I had just begun my first year of university on a scholarship. The abuse had taken place the summer before. I was going to put it all behind me and focus on the good that the Lord had opened up for me, but my first required course changed all of that for me.

I walked into the lecture hall, and the professor looked just like an older version of my abuser—the tone of his voice and speech pattern were exactly the same! I tried to change my schedule. I tried to take the course through another professor. It just didn't happen. I had to keep taking this course, which would have already been very difficult even without this challenge, since numbers were not my strength and I truly would have hated statistics even if this horrible situation had not presented itself! That year I lost my scholarship, since this one course caused me to lose my straight-A status.

I lost much more than that, though. It was a dark year for me. I lost myself. I hung tightly to God, but I felt like an empty shell holding on to the Lord. I became a different person. I was hiding, even from God. I was holding on to Him but not looking at Him. I appeared to have it all together, but inside and outside everything was falling apart. I was getting sick, but the doctors couldn't find anything wrong and told my parents in effect, "There's nothing we can do. There's nothing physically wrong with her that we can find. This must be something psychological." I couldn't hold on to this secret any longer. It was killing me and changing me into a person I didn't want to be.

I decided to make a visit to some dear friends who'd had a significant spiritual impact in my life, but had moved a few hours away. They knew me. They loved me. I knew this to be true. Seeking out people who can pray for me and have spiritual wisdom to share has been a life pattern and discipline of mine. It took me a little longer with this situation, but I knew it had to be done! Although the result wasn't anything that either of us expected, I know that they were right to have me unload this secret and share it with my family. I know that this was God working in me. He was teaching me to be totally open with Him and others. He was working on me, and I was learning to trust Him in the process of a lengthy journey. Without going into all the details, I will say this: Being open and vulnerable can come with a cost. It is painful, but with the pain comes healing if we allow it.

> Being open and vulnerable can come with a cost. It is painful, but with the pain comes healing if we allow it.

I told my family. I told one of my closest friends. What I got in response to my truth was blame. I think the question was, "What did you do to make this happen? This doesn't happen to good, Christian girls, and Christian men don't just do this." In this moment, all the lessons and sermons that I had been taught on forgiveness were challenging my obedience. It is very easy to forgive when you don't have to, when there is nothing yet to forgive. But real forgiveness is a process. It was a choice I had made before that day and have made over and over since then, concerning this situation and many others.

I had to forgive my abuser. I had to forgive my family. I knew they loved me, and I know they still do. Hurt people hurt people, and humans are not always good at handling disappointment. If Jesus could forgive from the cross, I had to forgive. There was no other passage to freedom, healing, or right relationship with God, and I wasn't willing to give that up!

And forgive us our debts, As we forgive our debtors… For if you forgive men their trespasses, your heavenly Father will also forgive you. But if you do not forgive men their trespasses, neither will your Father forgive your trespasses. (Matthew 6:12, 14-15)

I had to forgive me. I had to forgive myself for not being stronger. I had to forgive myself for allowing it to go on so long. I had to forgive myself for having head knowledge, but not the boldness to do what I knew to be right. I had to forgive God. Strange to have to forgive God since He and His ways are perfect, yet as much as I loved God, I was angry and disappointed that He let all of this happen. How could He be so good and not stop this? How could He be so good and allow my family to blame me? How could He be so good and allow me to finally share my secret, only to regret doing it? I heard it once said somewhere that we don't look to our circumstances to answer the question of whether God is good; we need only look to the cross when there is doubt. The cross automatically answers that question. So I cried, prayed, and praised at the foot of the cross.

I found God again. He is so good. He brought forgiveness to my life and healing to my heart.

Chapter Five
LORD, I WANT TO SEE YOU!

My father knew the city like the back of his hand. We had so many adventures on the subways and street cars. It seemed like every weekend, we travelled somewhere. We travelled a lot by transit. It was probably by necessity, but to me it was planned fun. I should have the stations memorized by now. No one needed a map when my dad was around. There was no GPS system back then, except for my father! It was amazing what he had stored in his memory.

We took in carnivals and exhibits. We met lots of people. Even now my dad always asks me if I remember such and such a person or some event, and I have no clue who or what he is talking about. Our childhood was always busy, filled with all sorts of places and people from all walks of life. I remember the walks to the corner store to get a weekly treat. I remember the design and tiles at a certain subway station. I remember family parties in our basement. I remember throwing up on a person on the subway—funny for me, but not so much for them! I said we travelled a lot by transit, but I didn't say I was good at it. I have always had motion sickness.

I am thankful to God that travelling back in time to most of these memories is heartwarming and feels like a breath of fresh air, even if the details are not all so clear. My dad could describe details and people with such precision. He saw things we didn't see. What a memory!

"Is your father blind?" It's a question I get all the time! The way my father engages in conversation and looks at people has them fooled. You would never know he was blind. I may have been too young to notice, or maybe my parents hid it well, but I didn't know there was a problem until we went on a trip to the Canadian National Institute for the Blind with my dad, and he didn't return home with us. We had weekly visits there for a while. Dad was learning a new way of life, and so were we.

My mom changed. She worried more. She worked more. My dad changed. He feared more. We went out less. I grew up fast and had more responsibility.

When my father lost his sight to glaucoma, it became a family problem in that my older sister and I had to be tested for it too. We were found to have the same condition, and needed to be monitored and treated so that we would not have the same fate as my father. From the very early age of about ten until into our twenties when our ophthalmologist retired, we went yearly to Mount Sinai Hospital to do tests and have our eyes checked.

I really disliked having my head strapped to the field test machine, having to look straight ahead without blinking, and trying to see what was in my peripheral view. I remember having to follow a bright light and press the button when it appeared. After a while I made it a fun challenge to conquer. It was a contest and I couldn't wait to see how I did. It seemed like such a long test back then. Now technology has come a long way, and it doesn't take so long anymore. I hated those pupil-opening, sticky yellow drops that made us unable to function for the rest of the day! Things were so wide and close that they looked blurry. I still hate those drops!

I remember thinking after each appointment, "Lord, I want my sight. I don't ever want to lose it. If this is just momentary visual impairment and I feel this way, what does my father feel like, not being able to see his children or his wife anymore? How does he feel not being able to experience colour or the beauty of the earth You created, which he used to know so well?" I can close my eyes and turn off the lights and think I know what it is to experience darkness, and yet I have no clue! I thank God that He has saved us, and that we never have to experience total darkness.

I remember one prayer meeting so vividly like it was yesterday. I still ask if it was real or just a vision. My father was in the middle of the circle being prayed for. They were praying specifically for his sight to return—and it did! Even for a brief moment, my father saw. I don't know why it didn't stay that way; I just know that in that moment I believed that if God could do it once, He could do it again.

I continue to pray today for Dad's eyes to be healed. I wouldn't be honest if I said that I never question God as to the reason for this, and yet things remain the way they've been for years. But having experienced what happened to Dad at the prayer meeting won't allow me to give up on having that prayer answered in the affirmative. It keeps me going to God with persistence. God's Word says He is a healing God. He does answer prayer. I am still waiting. Pray. Praise. Cry. Read and receive the Word. Repeat. I will continue to wait.

Here's another moment forever etched in my memory. It was an absolutely perfect day! The sun shone brightly, and at times became a little overcast. Perfect for pictures. It was 26 degrees Celsius. My prayers were answered. I held on to my daddy's arm. He was proud. I was happy! I took the lead, guiding him, but he led the way down the aisle. The music was heavenly. We stood together and just worshipped with everyone. I couldn't have asked for more!

As a little girl or teenager, you dream of your wedding day and your daddy walking you down the aisle. It was no different for me. I just prayed that God would heal and open his eyes. It broke my heart to think that my father wouldn't see his daughter as a bride. But on my day, I was just so happy he was there, so happy he could share it with me. I dreamed of my daddy walking me down the aisle and he did. I am sure that in his imagination I was the most beautiful sight of the day! As we worshipped that day, I knew it didn't matter that his physical eyes couldn't see me, because our hearts together saw and experienced God. It was the best part of my ceremony.

> *Wait on the Lord; Be of good courage, And He shall strengthen your heart; Wait, I say, on the Lord!* (Psalm 27:14)

I thank God that even in physical blindness, we can have spiritual sight. As I look back on this experience, I recognize my own desire to cry out to the Lord and tell Him, "I want to see You!"

I want to see You working. I don't want anything to be obstructing my view of You and what You are doing. I also don't want to see more than I need to and miss You altogether! Keep me focussed on You. Keep me looking for You and finding You. Keep me following Your light! Like that vision field test from my childhood, I want to conquer the journey while seeing the light that lights my way.

Your word is a lamp to my feet
And a light to my path. (Psalm 119:105)

In that moment, like so many others, I found God again. He is so good. He continues to walk with me and light my way.

Chapter Six
SOUNDS OF MUSIC

The sights and sounds were new every morning. The scenery took my breath away. What a testament to the glory of God. I couldn't believe my eyes! We had been in beautiful, warm, sunny weather down below, and suddenly the air became crisp and the peaks covered with snow. It was a beautiful picture! I was (and still am) afraid of heights, but I couldn't miss this chance. I'm glad I didn't! Switzerland was beautiful. So was Austria. The lush green grass rolled with the wind, like notes moving smoothly across a score.

We connected with the people heart to heart, even though we couldn't speak a word to each other. Germany and the Czech Republic were just as beautiful. This was a trip of a lifetime! I was so blessed that the Lord had granted me this opportunity. We had worked and practiced a year to take the message of Christ to this part of the world. The preparation had been a lot of work, but I was ready.

I was surprised by so many expressions of God's greatness. God revealed Himself through nature, and the earth really praised God. The beauty our eyes beheld was beyond words. My photos couldn't do it justice. Being a part of what God was doing—

using us to make a difference in the lives of people around the world—will be forever imprinted in my memory and heart. It was a humbling experiencing. We laughed. We cried. We prayed. We tried new things. We shared meals. We connected. God used us to bless the people, and the people in turn blessed us.

I still laugh when I think about it. I had left Canada to sing, but I nearly didn't return: I was even given a marriage proposal! Of course, I didn't give it a second thought—except to humour myself. While backstage, a gentleman I had never seen before tried to kiss me and invited me to join his harem. God has a sense of humour! He was finding a way to imprint lasting joy in my heart.

Although this trip had gotten off to a slow start, it was starting to produce some very happy memories. It was a dream come true. I was so glad to be in the moment. God had made it happen.

YOU ARE THE AIR I BREATHE

Perhaps it was the basement apartment I had lived in during my third year of university, or maybe the stresses of life made this problem bigger than it needed to be, but I had a few years of very bad asthma attacks. I had watched my brother suffer as a child with asthma, and it hadn't been a pretty sight. It had affected our whole family and all our day-to-day activities. We'd gone for many hospital visits and returned home lugging the oxygen machine. Our family had gone through a lot with my brother's condition.

There was never a sign that I would later struggle with asthma. While I'd had many other health issues to deal with, asthma hadn't been one of them until now. Just when I felt I was getting my life back together and getting back on track with school, asthma hit me like a ton of bricks. I had just been celebrating God's goodness in allowing me to get into the Concurrent Education Teaching Degree program, and I figured there was no way God would allow me to have another year of confusion—not after my first year's experience.. He had worked a miracle by getting me into this program—I knew that it had been God Who had opened that door for me. But even that miracle did not prevent this storm!

I went in for many hospital tests. There were, many infections. Many prescriptions, and many missed days of classes and placement. Many questions and much confusion! I just wanted to breathe. I wanted to stop having pain and constriction in my chest. I wanted to stop coughing. I wanted answers. "I need to succeed this year! What is the reason for this battle? Please fix this!" I prayed. I praised. I cried. I read and received the Word. Repeat.

The answer I got was that I lived because Christ lived in me. It was truly in Him that I moved and breathed. Every day was a gift from God. My asthma troubles followed me to Europe, even though we had prayed many times before leaving and during the trip. But during one of our performances, I fainted and had to be carried off the stage. A gentleman who claimed to be a doctor came to help, and then the moment came that I will never forget—the marriage proposal.

The whole trip was plagued with asthma attacks and challenges for me. But I did see God at work. It's in challenging times like these that we see God's strength make our weaknesses seem just that: weak against God's power!

And He said to me, "My grace is sufficient for you, for My strength is made perfect in weakness." (2 Corinthians 12:9, NKJV)

I don't even know how it was figured out, but in the midst of this madness someone looked at the medication I was using for my eyes and the inhaler medication and realized that one affected the other. I had to stop the glaucoma medication if I wanted to breathe! God used this experience to teach me a very valuable lesson: Sometimes what used to be helpful for us needs to be removed. Sometimes what used to work may not work anymore. Sometimes we are looking at the wrong solution to fix many problems. One thing affects another. Nothing happens in isolation.

This is so true about our relationship with God. He truly does work in mysterious ways. He also takes what looks like a mess and makes a life map out of it. God really does work all things together for our good. It still doesn't all make sense to me, but I do know that I need to just let Him lead and be my very breath.

> Sometimes what used to be helpful for us needs to be removed. Sometimes what used to work may not work anymore. Sometimes we are looking at the wrong solution to fix many problems.

This was such a time of busyness. It couldn't be helped—life just took over, and I had to fight so many things. I had to fight to keep up with the workload from school. I had to fight to work while battling illnesses, doctor's appointments, and the class and placement workloads. I had to prepare for the missions trip. I thought I was in love. Ha! The truth was that although I trusted God, I forgot to let Him fight for me in this season. I began fighting by myself. I didn't allow myself to rest in Him. I thought I was giving Him all my cares, but I kept picking them up, and this only added to my health issues.

God reminds me many times that I need to stop myself from taking in the wrong air if I want to breathe properly. I need to check out the pollution in my space and clear the room. I often have to be reminded to slow down and evaluate. Am I taking my directives from too many people, and not taking the time to inhale and exhale God's presence?

The solution was such an easy one, and yet it eluded us all. I worried much and went from one medical appointment to another, accepting the doctor's reports. But God had the answer all along. I found God again. He is so good. He revealed truth and provided wisdom. He was a shelter in the time of storm.

Chapter Seven
HEART OF WORSHIP

Rehearsals were our own private concerts. Warmups felt like the actual performance at times. We sang with all our hearts on Friday nights. People could have walked in off the street and felt like they were at one of our concerts—I'm sure they heard us from outside and didn't have to come in! God was truly with us during these times, as we clapped and stomped and danced and swayed. The music filled the sanctuary and the basement. The prayer times at rehearsals were just another way of singing.

I will never forget these moments. As I clapped my hands and moved my feet, I watched the hands of our amazingly talented—but, more importantly, committed—conductor, showing us when we were to do this or do that. She was committed to God and to this ministry. Despite my close attention, I knew what was going to happen next with my eyes closed! The melody in my heart kept going, and drew me into God's arms of love every time.

I remember being in rehearsal as the piano keys started—it was one of my favourite songs being played. The words of the song were exactly what I needed to hear from the Lord, and He spoke. God was the strength of my life. He was my portion.

The praise and worship portions of Sunday services are my favourite! I feel like I'm dancing on a cloud and in my own world when music begins to play. I get transported to another dimension when the notes of the instruments and the sounds of the voices begin to mix together. I love worship! In these two experiences through the choir and corporate praise and worship, I couldn't be happier. God allows me to be in His presence through song, and it is rich. He is so close in those moments!

There is nothing worse than wanting to sing because you enjoy it and because God has gifted you to do so, and then finding out that you can't. I remember when I was told that there were nodules on my vocal chords that had to be removed, and that I wouldn't be able to sing for a whole year if I ever expected to sing again. I was part of the Toronto Mass Choir at the time. I was also in my church choir and did solo music ministry. How could this be happening? No amount of praying, praising, or crying changed my reality. I feel close to God when worshipping. How was I to keep getting close to God now? What was I going to do? How did I get here?

I was also a teacher. How do you teach without speaking? In this period of my life, God was showing me my own heart. Yes, I loved God. Yes, I loved the opportunity of ministering in music, but God was asking me an important question: if He took away all that He had blessed me with—something I was using to bless others with, and that I greatly enjoyed—would I still worship Him?

I thought I was good at what I did, but I had a lot to learn! I still do. I also learned that worship was not only about the music, but it is about my life and heart. It was in this season that I began to learn how to truly hear Him say, *"Be still and know that I am God"* (Psalm 46:10). It was in this season that I began to know what it was to listen to God speak to me in so many other ways.

During that year, I stood in practice and sang with my heart. I listened with my heart as well as my ears. I learned my parts, although I could not voice them. But I was still worshipping God! The Spirit was working in my heart and life.

God is Spirit, and those who worship Him must worship in spirit and truth. (John 4:24)

My heart was being prepared to lead others in worship, and I couldn't do that without knowing the heart of worship. Some lessons in life really hurt. This was one of them for me. In this lesson, it wasn't about my voice. It wasn't about the music. God wanted all of me. I thought I was giving Him that, but He revealed to me that I wasn't. I needed to present myself to God as a living sacrifice, and that was my spiritual act of worship.

I didn't know then if I would get a voice back to sing, but I still needed to worship Him with whatever He gave me and in spite of what might be taken away. There were many days spent in the cycle that I have followed so many times without change: Pray. Praise. Cry. Read and receive the Word. Repeat. Those were the days of a broken and contrite heart, and God accepted it.

> ...but I still needed to worship Him with whatever He gave me and in spite of what might be taken away.

This is still the case. Today, I worship in more humility as I think of the grace God has extended. God broke me then—gracefully. He allowed something I held very dear to be taken from me. I was glad that I didn't hold on to it too tightly. I knew that God loved me, and I had no choice but to consider the possibility, through my tears, that I might not be given my voice back. I had to come to the truth that this gift was exactly that: a gift. God knew what He had planned for me. He was going to leave me with what I needed to accomplish what He wanted. God was looking to create in me His image.

His purpose is conformity more than comfort. He allowed this trouble to bring that about. It was done in His love because of love. Sometimes healing actually comes through suffering first.

I do have my voice, and I do love to use it to worship. I am thankful that God still wants it that way, too. I choose brokenness before God when it comes to worship now. It allows God to bring wholeness in worship that brings wholeness to my life. In my brokenness, I am complete. God can complete His work. I found God again. He is so good. He accepted my worship, and He gave me a song.

> His purpose is conformity more than comfort.

Chapter Eight
EMPTY YET FILLED!

The moment I was pregnant, I knew! I had felt the change within my body. I waited a couple of weeks before taking a test, but it only confirmed what I'd already known. We were so excited! I enjoyed watching the changes in my body and feeling the movement when the kicking started. I loved being pregnant. There is no experience in life that has shown me the power of God in such an intimate, detailed way.

When I think back now, the months went by quickly. I soon couldn't see my feet because my stomach was so big. From behind, you couldn't tell I was pregnant, but watch out world when I turned around! My boys look at my pictures and are amazed every time at how big I was. When I look at the pictures, I'm amazed too! It was a very exciting time in our lives.

Then, the big moment came. We heard the first cry. He snuggled into his father's arms and made himself comfortable there. We were so happy that he had arrived safely—our first beautiful gift from God. What a miracle!

The news of my second pregnancy three years later came as a surprise, since I'd recently had surgery. When our second miracle arrived, he, too, went to his father first. It must be a boy thing! Again, we were amazed at the miracle of life that God had blessed us with.

> *For you created my inmost being; you knit me together in my mother's womb. I praise you because I am fearfully and wonderfully made; your works are wonderful, I know that full well.* (Psalm 139:13–14, NIV)

We had reason to view our children as miracles. We hadn't even made it to our first year of marriage when I began to have severe female issues. We'd only been married a few months. I'd probably had these issues before, but marriage has a way of bringing out things you are unaware of.

I remember being in the doctor's office only to hear him say, "I don't think you will be able to have children. I'd like you to try now just so we can see what we are dealing with." We were newlyweds! We didn't plan on waiting long, but to have to try with the belief that it might not be possible is stressful to say the least. But God had other plans!

> *My frame was not hidden from You,*
> *When I was made in secret,*
> *And skillfully wrought in the lowest parts of the earth.*
> *Your eyes saw my substance, being yet unformed.*
> *And in Your book they all were written,*
> *The days fashioned for me,*
> *When as yet there were none of them.* (Psalm 139:15–16)

God proved the doctor wrong only four or five months after we were told it probably wasn't going to happen for us. I was sick from the moment I conceived, and remained sick until I gave birth. Each day was long. Each day was tiring. Each day was painful. I did ask many times, "Why are you letting this happen this way? God, don't you care about what's happening to me?" I prayed. I praised. I cried. I read and received the Word. Repeat. I gave God thanks because I was carrying life. I just kept telling myself that "this too shall pass." I had been given a gift, and I was going to hold my gift soon.

Both pregnancies gave me lots of trouble, and both deliveries were a nightmare in their own way. One took lots of doctors and instruments to encourage my son's entry into this world; the other put me into surgery. One was twenty-eight hours, and the other two days. One had a cord around his neck and wanted to come out the wrong side first; the other went into distress and had to be saved. One I didn't get to meet until hours later as I haemorrhaged and went unconscious; the other I also met later because they had to stitch me back up and let me rest. I stayed in the hospital for a week after both of them, but I was thanking God that I had babies to bring home.

Our lives have been full with them. I had always wanted to have four children, but after the difficult journey to have my boys, I let go of that wish for a while. Between the boys, I also had surgery and sickness that prevented me from thinking about more children, even if I had really wanted to make that dream a reality.

It was Mother's Day weekend. As a minister, I had a wedding to perform on Saturday. I had performed the rehearsal just two days before. The music at the rehearsal was so fun, and the bride was coming in on a plane. The wedding was taking place at an airport! This was going to be a fun, celebratory weekend. I'd never been to or done a wedding in an airport before—what an adventure it was going to be!

Then on Sunday, my family was going to gather at my home to celebrate all the moms in our lives. This was to be a full but good weekend—routine in some ways, as Mother's Day comes every year, but busy as that just seems to be the story of my life. I like busy. It keeps me out of trouble. The weekend was all planned out, and I was prepared—or so I thought. Then, something happened.

We decided on the spur of the moment that we would send the boys on an overnighter. I was so excited for my boys. They were coming home from school on Friday to go on their own adventure—a surprise sleepover! They came home from school, and we had their bags packed. The look of joy in their eyes as they found out where they were going and who was waiting for them allowed me to breathe a sigh of relief. Our surprise plan had worked!

I was lying on the couch when they came home. They were so happy to be going, they didn't even notice that I didn't get up. They ran over, kissed me, and just as fast as they came in, they went out. They were going to have an amazing evening. When they returned home the next day, they ran into the house to tell their stories of adventure. I was happy to see them, and they were happy to see me. Our plan had worked! At least for them. They were oblivious to the kind of adventure their dad and I had just had. I was glad about that.

While they'd been away, I had played music at home. I sang with it as much as I could. I mostly listened. This time it didn't comfort me, but it strengthened me. I cried. I prayed. I played music. Pray. Praise. Cry. Read and receive the Word. Repeat. Praising God truly had a way of taking me into a place of peace I otherwise wouldn't have had and desperately needed in that situation. This was what my boys had to see, to experience, to live in. The music created an atmosphere of peace.

The joy I'd anticipated just two days before had turned into great sorrow. I wasn't kept from trouble—I was walking right into it. So much for busy and celebrating! I was missing the wedding!

I'd wanted that experience. I'd wanted to keep my word. How could I let this bride and groom down?! The thoughts in my head were many, and the pain in my heart was great. But I am so thankful that God takes care of what we can't. He sent a colleague who did a perfect job. The couple even sent me a picture and thank you card. They told me they missed me and had me in their hearts. God also had my boys in safe care, and they were having a good time building memories.

Che and I were making memories of our own, holding onto each other and holding even tighter to God's hand. We were saying goodbye to our baby. I was having a miscarriage. We had just found out that I was expecting. I had been pregnant nearly three months unknowingly, but when we found out, we embraced the idea with great expectation and happiness. I was sure that this was my girl!

For my other two pregnancies, I'd been sick from the day of conception to the day of birth. Now the surprise that had tiptoed into our lives was stomping out. I went from carrying a baby to being a mom who would miss carrying this precious gift. Life asked us to say goodbye before we had even said hello. I don't know why God chose to give and then take away.

Sunday was a day that we were supposed to celebrate, and I was only going to be bringing a sacrifice of praise. Thank God— He does receive that. I know most people probably wouldn't have done what I did, but this was pretty normal for me. It's what I do, so it's what I did. I needed it. We got dressed as usual and made our way to church. I told myself the boys had to go to church, but really I was the one who needed to be there. It was going to be life as usual, and I needed to keep life as usual.

I don't even remember what the service was about. All I know is that I praised and prayed and cried and prayed. God held me. I did feel that. All of this probably sounds strange, as worship and grief are not what people typically pair together, but

I pair worship with my hurt often. I have learned to practice worshipping God no matter what is happening. It doesn't always feel good, although for me, this choice does come easy. For me, it works.

Worship didn't release me in that moment from the depth of pain that I was feeling. I still had to walk that road. But it transported me to a place where in the midst of the storm, God sheltered me in overwhelming peace—a peace I couldn't have found in any way other than seeking His presence. There He received my tears and held me close. My heart was broken in so many pieces. I knew that God could heal my broken heart, but I had to give it all to Him—every single piece.

The Lord gives and He takes away. His ways are higher, and I trust Him beyond my own understanding. I know He is working out the details of my life, connecting them for my good. I may not know how or always understand, but I leave it to Him. Going to church that day, I felt like David after he'd lost his son. He chose to worship God. Was there any other or better choice? I couldn't think of one.

Mother's Day dinner was enjoyed like any other. We shared a meal. We shared laughs. We shared love. I was surrounded by mothers, and I was a mother. I had the gift of my two boys. I had much to be thankful for. God had blessed me.

Six months later, we travelled the same road. We had another miscarriage. Once more I prayed. I praised. I cried. I read and received the Word. Repeat. "Why, Lord, am I experiencing this hurt?" I didn't get an aswer to that question, but God still met me.

The Lord is close to the brokenhearted and saves those who are crushed in spirit. (Psalm 34:18, NIV)

I am not the first, and I won't be the last to experience this pain. I know that God has used it to help me comfort others. I will meet my other two angels in heaven. I did get my wish: I did have four children. I just have to wait a little longer for a better introduction. Now every time I look at my boys I am reminded that I may be emptier than I had planned, but our lives remain so full. I found God again. He is so good. He brought comfort.

Chapter Nine
IN YOU I MOVE

I never thought I'd like the gym. I surprised myself, and it was now part of my normal routine. It was exciting for me to set goals and to reach them. I discovered my love of Zumba. I discovered that I liked feeling strong and growing muscles. Being able to go to the gym three or four times a week gave me more energy than I thought possible.

Keeping a routine and working out is hard work, even if it is fun. The commitment to it, though, brings results that you don't regret and wouldn't return! I was glad I'd embraced this newfound activity. I needed this in my life! This was a season to try new things.

In another new venture, my arms waved and my feet moved side to side. The room was filled with smiles. I was so glad I had been exercising—I was using all my energy! I couldn't help but be a charismatic leader. The choir sounded clear. The melodies rung out, and they were true instruments of praise. I was excited by what God had produced with my efforts. I learned that I enjoyed conducting. It was fun, although it was also a lot of hard work. This choir was a true testament of God's faithfulness. I was glad to have been used by God once again. I needed this in my life, too!

In many seasons in my life, I've had to work hard to stay well. I've had to work hard physically, emotionally, mentally and spiritually. It was work all around for me, and it had to be done daily. This was one of those seasons.

For in him we live and move and have our being... We are his offspring. (Acts 17:28, NIV)

For years I suffered with bone pain, muscle aches, knee problems, and migraines, and they seemed to have been leading to this period in my life. It could also have been the major car accident I had just before going into my first year of teaching, or the three or four others I'd had afterwards, which were beginning to show hidden effects years later. One would think I didn't know how to drive, but in every case I wasn't at fault. Satan really has been out to kill me.

There is no other way to explain some things except in the spiritual sense, and to know that the supernatural hand of God has been working to save me! Two of the car accidents I had were a real testament to that.

In the first case, I was on my way to a choir rehearsal one evening. I had just passed an intersection when I felt and heard a loud hard hit to the driver's side of my car. A lady coming from the opposite direction had decided that she needed to make a left turn right into me. I don't know what happened in those moments. Voices were heard as if I was under water. There were sirens and people. There was me, bleeding and in shock. There was the loss of feeling in my body. There were the Jaws of Life to get me out of the car.

I was rushed to the hospital, and there was no one in my family who could be reached—they were all at different prayer meetings. In fact, I found out later that in one such meeting, someone felt that I needed to be prayed for, that I was in trouble. God was already working on my behalf! I was finally able to have EMS get through to a friend who came for me.

After much testing, the doctors said I was lucky to have gotten out of this accident in the condition that I did. My feeling returned, and they couldn't find any major problems—bruising and whiplash, a cracked rib and an injured wrist, but nothing that therapy wouldn't fix. My family had no idea what had happened that night until a friend brought me home early the next morning. They'd all been at all-night prayer meetings! They were so surprised to see the state I was in, but their prayers had saved me from a worse fate. I had a solo that Sunday morning at church and a concert that weekend with the choir. I did sing with a neck brace on, but I worshipped with all my heart! I never got my car back. It was a total write-off.

In another incident, I was driving to an early morning choir meeting. We were going on a trip, and we had to meet the bus. I had two other members in the car with me. I thank God that the highway was clear, because all of a sudden the car decided to drive itself. It didn't matter that my foot was on the brakes. It wouldn't stop. All we could think of doing was to cry out to God for help. He directed me to turn off at the next exit. The car was going at such a high speed that we thought we would surely meet our Maker that day. Yet as I turned off, there was a gas station to my right. I turned in there, we closed our eyes and screamed, and I pulled the key out. The car stopped, inches away from hitting the building!

We left the car there that weekend. Someone picked us up, and we got to the bus on time and worshipped all weekend with the choir. We were walking miracles. Turns out the car had a faulty message system. The message it was getting wasn't what I was sending!

I look back on this memory and think about the years that I had so many physical issues that didn't make sense. My body wasn't getting the message that I wanted it to go in a different direction and be well. I was steering it one way, and it was going another. The systems in my body were running at their own speed: fast and furious!

There was one year where five doctors at three hospitals saw a lot of me. They all thought they were treating separate things until one doctor connected the dots. I was seeing a rheumatologist, an ENT (ear, nose, and throat) specialist, an integrative medicine specialist, a gynaecologist, and another doctor whose specialty I'd never even heard of! The appointments filled my life with so much stress. I spent consecutive months on antibiotics. I woke up with serious vertigo. My body was always in pain and swelling up. There was always a feeling of exhaustion. I was having procedures done that I'd never heard of before! There were a lot of things happening all at once. Why couldn't they find what was wrong?

I remember asking, "God, why aren't You showing the answer? Why are there so many things wrong and so many symptoms?" I went for so many tests. I didn't know that so much blood could be taken at once: in a single occasion, I had over eighteen vials taken. The waits in the hospital took up so much of my day that I could barely manage to be a mom and a wife. They thought I might have MS. They thought I might have lupus. I was told I had a disease called lichen sclerosus, which is a skin rash disease that can lead to cancer. So many questions. I had been on a similar journey like this before. It was déjà vu! There was only one way to handle this. Pray. Praise. Cry. Read and receive the Word. Repeat.

It was during this time that Che was laid off! "Lord, how? Why now?" *Yet,* this was God providing exactly what we needed. Che being home for almost four years helped us to navigate the world of confusion that surrounded us. As I have shared before, God truly provided in miraculous ways during this time! Che went back to school, and was paid to do so. I had Che's help at home because his schedule was flexible, and he could help take me to my appointments or even be home with the boys. We had lots of help from family. It wasn't easy financially or physically, but there was still much to be thankful for. I surprisingly continued to go to the gym—a little less, but I kept going. I conducted the choir! I eased back into work at the church and in teaching. I didn't always feel good, but I felt God with me and accomplished all He wanted me to do. Through it all, we had to exercise my spiritual cycle—Pray. Praise. Cry. Read and receive the Word. Repeat!

But the Lord is faithful, and he will strengthen you and protect you from the evil one. (2 Thessalonians 3:3, NIV)

Praise the Lord, my soul; all my inmost being, praise his holy name. Praise the Lord, my soul, and forget not all his benefits—who forgives your sins and heals all your diseases, who redeems your life from the pit and crowns you with love and compassion, who satisfies your desires with good things so that your youth is renewed like the eagle's. (Psalm 103:1–5, NIV)

The doctors couldn't figure out why all of this was happening. They also couldn't figure out why my tests were showing that something was certainly wrong in my immune system, but I wasn't presenting like someone who had all the various things they were diagnosing. I was given the label of an "unknown autoimmune disease," as well as arthritis and fibromyalgia. There came a point in this exercise of madness that I decided that this wasn't what I wanted to be doing. I wanted activity that was going to make me better, and I wasn't going to settle for anything less. My doctor's appointments became fewer and fewer, as I refused to take the drugs they wanted to give. As they studied me, although the results were showing something different, I was displaying greater health. The Word of God was at work in my life, and improved life was coming back to me. God was daily loading me with benefits and renewing my strength. I found God again. He is so good. He continued to touch me.

Chapter Ten

A TIME FOR TEA

A friend loves at all times… (Proverbs 17:17, NIV)

Sometimes a nice cup of tea and wonderful prayer with a friend make life so beautiful. It is the simple, small things in life that truly remind us that God loves us so intimately. He attends to the small details. God designed us to be in fellowship and community with others. I am so thankful that God continues to reveal that He is a relational God, in this way and others. I am a social person, and God has given me some dear friends with whom I can be myself anytime.

I think of visiting one friend. Sitting in her living room gives me calm and peace. The sun brightens the space through the big window at the front of her room, bringing me comfort every time I am there. I love her sense of style. She is great with her decor and is so hospitable. I think of these as gifts—both her sense of style, and how she opens her home to others. I need that gift, and I take it all in as we sit in quiet for a bit or laugh like mature schoolgirls. I take in the painting on the wall and the colours of the room. It changes a lot, and I always love it. Even small changes like the cushions make such a difference. I always wish she would come live with me and be my interior designer. These thoughts bring silent laughter to my heart. I study the fireplace. I spend time looking outside and studying the tree in the front yard.

God gives me a thought. I am so grateful when God uses the little things in our surroundings to speak to us of the bigness of who He is! The welcoming presence in her home, the calm tone of her voice, the tree outside and how it is still standing after battling many storms, the light of the sun breaking through the leaves outside into where we are sitting, a cup of tea, taking the time to just be still in the moment—these are all gifts that tell me God welcomes me and God really does love me. God uses human ways to speak and bring comfort, even without human words. God is present in the storms of life, and we make it through because of Him. The sun shines even through the clouds! His light penetrates everything. We can stop and receive small blessings that warm our hearts even in moments when we think there is no blessing to be found. If we look to Him with gratitude, we can see Him working things out for our good. If we look hard enough, we see God using things for His glory.

Are you ever thankful for the people God chooses for you? God puts people in our lives, and through those relationships shows Himself faithful yet again! This friend and I first connected because she was a pastor at a church I attended. We became lasting friends soon thereafter—thirteen years now. The fact that I can just pick up the phone and she is available and ready to receive me is a blessing from God. Most times it is for no particular reason—just because. Just because we want to. Just because she wants to mentor me. Just because we share common interests. Just because we want to pray for each other. Just because we want to do something fun, and that might be connecting and talking. Just because we are women. In fact,

God has given me a few sisters like this. I enjoy tea with all of them. Through difficult times, I am blessed to have a tribe of women I can count on! Good thing I love tea, because there is always time for a tea party.

Chapter Eleven
NO ORDINARY WORK DAY

It started off as an ordinary work day. I had planned my week's classes, and the following week I was going to be having surgery. I was feeling relaxed and happy. Everything was in order. This year's classes were challenging. In fact, the last few years had been! It seemed as if it was the norm now for every year to be a little more difficult than the last, so I was feeling very thankful that I was at peace and my morning had started out stress-free. My class was having a very happy time with instruments when my vice principal walked in. She was her usual chipper self. I thought she was just observing and visiting. She asked to speak with me, saying our other VP needed to see me. One of our EAs came to take over the class.

We walked the hallway to his office, carrying on with small talk. It was a hallway I walked daily. The music and melody of little three- to five-year-old voices in deep tones and high pitches, greeting me with "Hi Mrs. Spencer," filled the air. As we passed classrooms, the squeezes of little arms around my thighs because they couldn't reach my waist (even with me being as short as I am) felt good. There was a calm in the midst of the busyness. All was right.

We arrived at his office. I had no idea why I was there. I'd sat in this office many times, as we had a great relationship. We joked about many things—food, music, the love of arts, our families, religion, and so many other aspects of life! We shared deep life struggles as well. His office was always a welcoming space. When I entered, nothing felt out of the ordinary until he opened his mouth.

I saw his lips moving, but I don't know when I stopped hearing him. All I know is that he passed the phone and said I could call my husband. I heard myself saying, "Honey, I have just been accused of physical misconduct, and I will be escorted out of school and sent back home."

The walk back to my class to get my belongings was the same walk I had just taken, yet its silence was now screaming at me. I didn't hear the voices. I didn't feel the gentle squeezes of the children. I was numb. My VPs tried to make me feel loved and supported. We moved about quickly, yet with discretion. No one knew what had just happened to me. But in an instant, a perfect storm had just come and left wreckage that no one else could see.

They walked me to the door. and told me they knew I would be fine. I had been teaching for eighteen years. They knew me. I was the resident staff "pastor." My nickname was "the Rev." I had their support, even though until the investigation was completed, I couldn't be in contact with them or anyone else from the school. They gave me numbers to call and hugged me. I walked to my car and sat for what seemed like forever. It was surreal!

I called a friend as I didn't want to go home and be left in silence with my thoughts and shock. I needed a cup of tea!

She had a cup of tea for me. We prayed. We talked, and God ministered to me. I realized that He already had the situation all worked out while I was having my tea. My phone rang. The officer in charge of my case called to assure me that although there was a procedure to follow, he had been told of my reputation and all was going to be well. It would go no further than this. I could relax and breathe.

How gracious of God to send me this message. He was taking what the devil had intended for evil and turning it into something good. I could only rejoice and be thankful for the rest that God was about to give me. I had surgery coming the following week, and all I could think was that God felt my body needed rest before it and time to recover during the weeks after. I was now going to have this time off without losing pay or sick days! I could focus on healing, and that was exactly what I was going to do.

> *"No weapon formed against you shall prosper,*
> *And every tongue which rises up against you in judgment*
> *You shall condemn.*
> *This is the heritage of the servants of the Lord,*
> *And their righteousness is from me,"*
> *Says the Lord.* (Isaiah 54:17)

We continued to enjoy our tea and our visit. I was at peace, so much so that I called my tribe of women and retold the story from a place of power and victory. They were in shock, but I had joy unspeakable.

> *…rejoicing in hope, patient in tribulation, continuing steadfastly in prayer…* (Romans 12:12)

God was working. I just needed to let Him do the work while I enjoyed the time.

Sometimes shock takes longer to wear off than you expect. I must have been in survival mode after my surgery, because as I recovered it hit me that I had been wrongfully accused of something terrible. I was very glad to be away from school to heal, and in that regard it was a blessing that this process was taking as long as it did. But with that time came guilt, anger, sadness, shame, grief. My good teaching record was in question. My walk of integrity was in question. There were some I had confided in who questioned my actions when the resolution was taking longer than expected. While I was seeing God working and releasing me to rest and grow in other areas of my life during this time, others that I thought would support me saw it as a problem.

God had already told me that all was going to be well, but the time it took for that to happen almost made me forget the message. Sometimes it's hard to believe what God has said when living in the moments before the fulfillment of the answer. When reality looks so different from the truth of God's Word, I sometimes become weak. In this situation, I wanted to be a woman like Sarah:

...she considered him faithful who made the promise.
(Hebrews 11:11b, NIV)

I practiced my regular routine. It had served me well before, and I knew it would not fail me now, so I spent my days in prayer, in praise, crying, and reading and receiving the Word. Repeat. Of course, I also spent some days having tea and praying with my tribe of trusted friends. Thank God for friends that bring warmth, sweetness and comfort to my days—just like a good cup of tea. I had to remind my soul that God's message was going to come to pass. They reminded me, too!

So shall my Word be that goes forth from My mouth;
It shall not return to Me void,

But it shall accomplish what I please,
And it shall prosper in the thing for which I sent it. (Isaiah 55:11)

God was going to prosper me. I wasn't going to have a bad record or trouble adjusting when I returned to school. I had to quiet the voices trying to whisper a different message to my brain. During tough times, especially the ones that last awhile, the devil lies to you, saying things like, "God doesn't love you. God has forgotten you. God doesn't care. God isn't going to help you. God has changed His mind." The devil is the father of lies. He tried to use my vulnerability to have me question the power of God. I couldn't let Satan cause me to question what God had already decided to take care of for me. Pray. Praise. Cry. Read and receive the Word. Repeat.

Cast your burden on the Lord,
And He shall sustain you;
He shall never permit the righteous to be moved. (Psalm 55:22)

I was solid in the Lord. I was going to be just fine. No matter what anyone else said, thought, or didn't say, I was going to trust the Lord. I didn't know why He had allowed this experience to be part of my story, and I still wonder, but I know I won't understand the reasons for everything, so I am to trust God in all things.

I tried to go back to work that year. I lasted a couple of weeks, and then I knew that I needed to allow God to heal me. My body and heart and mind had been through so much. The surgery was still taking its toll on my body. The student who had accused me was still in the class I had to teach. I needed a break. Since I hadn't used up my sick days, I now had those to use. Wow! I couldn't have worked it out any better. God, You are so good!

Trust in the Lord with all your heart,
And lean not on your own understanding;
In all your ways acknowledge Him,
And He shall direct your paths. (Proverbs 3:5–6, NKJV)

I found God. He is so good. He was my Defender and Protector. He led the way, and He surrounded me with friendship.

Chapter Twelve
IT'S BEGINNING TO LOOK
A LOT LIKE CHRISTMAS

Christmas is one of my family's favourite times of year. We all look forward to Christmas morning. I looked around the room at the excited faces of my boys. This morning, they didn't want us to rush the story to get to the gifts. Instead, we took our time through our tradition. We read the various aspects of the Christmas story and between each chapter sang our favourite carols. Each moment in time brought the boys closer to me as they snuggled in where we all could fit under the blanket on the couch. The truth of God's love was so real to us. The blessing of sharing in God's love by being together couldn't be taken for granted. I searched the room and took in everything in slow motion. I wanted these memories imprinted on my heart. God had been so good to us! The boys were growing so fast.

As soon as the gifts were opened, we continued on to our next tradition—breakfast! They boys wanted to do it this time. I was just supposed to instruct them, and they would make it all happen. Homemade waffles were my specialty, but they insisted that there was no time like the present for them to learn. So I gave the instructions, and they got to work! My kitchen was a disaster, but my heart was full before my tummy got a chance to be. *A Charlie Brown Christmas* played. The boys sang and danced as breakfast creations surfaced. It looked like Christmas. It sounded like Christmas. It smelled like Christmas. It felt like Christmas in that perfect moment.

I remember our evening spent with extended family and friends at my sister's. The carol "Silent Night" kept ringing through my ears. It was a pretty quiet and very peaceful night. The Christmas lights seemed picture perfect. I felt as if I was in a dream, and I was so blessed by the sounds of laughter and joy. There truly were tidings of comfort and joy all around, although it was a much quieter Christmas than usual. Some are like that. Some blessings and gifts leave us speechless. All was well.

I thank God that He uses the positive memories to ease the discomfort of the painful ones. How I just recalled Christmas is the way I like to remember it. That memory is my home away from home. But not every Christmas has been so joyful.

It had happened so fast. We were celebrating Che's birthday and my parent's anniversary. I couldn't really do much as I had just had surgery the week before, so I ate some cake and was planning on going to bed. The boys had gone out for an early dinner and now they were going to a movie. They left with so much excitement—or perhaps it was the sugar rush from some amazing home-made carrot cake with the best cream cheese icing! Mom and Dad left shortly after to go home. I was excited that I had a friend dropping by to drop off a Christmas hamper for a family I really wanted to bless. God again proved Himself so intimate with the details of His timing! She came, and I had to be rushed to hospital.

When I stood up, fluid started pouring out of my body as if my water had just broke—except that there was no way that was possible! I was surely not pregnant, since the surgery I'd just had was a hysterectomy. The person on the Telehealth phone line told me to get to Emergency, so off we went.

My friend stayed with me until we could reach Che after the movie. I knew what was happening, since I hadn't been feeling well all week and thought something was wrong. That was the second trip I had made to the Emergency that week. I had also gone to see my specialist, but the tests came back negative. I did my own research, and what took them days to discover was only a confirmation to me.

They sent me home with instructions to see another specialist first thing in the morning. That was Dec 23rd. I was sent back to the hospital and spent the day again in Emergency, only to be admitted for surgery that night. I never got to see my boys, and all of a sudden they were being shared between my brother and sister. I can't imagine what they were going through. As I came out from surgery we were told it hadn't worked, and I would need to have another one on Christmas Eve. So that morning I went for another procedure—to be tubed in my kidney. I begged to go home so my boys could see me and have Christmas. The medical workers monitored me all day and made arrangements for home care. I got home at 11:30 p.m., and my boys were returned to me.

When the door opened they ran to me, and I hugged and kissed them. In their reality, one day I was there and the next I was not. How hard it must have been for them to hear that I was in the hospital again and having surgery! My youngest just couldn't keep it together anymore. He broke down screaming and crying. It was a moment I will remember forever.

God brought us together and saved our Christmas. I spent most of the day on the couch medicated and in pain. I rested, but I was present. I rested in the strong hug of baby Jesus and the soft touches of my boys. Peace on earth and goodwill were my personal experience that Christmas. I prayed. I praised. I cried. Repeat. Immanuel—God with us—joined me in my experience. I was so blessed. I found God. He is so good. He made a way where there was no way.

Chapter Thirteen
WORSHIP IN THE WAR

Music is a gift—at least, it is to me. I listen to it. I sing it. I play it. I twist and shout! It is my "go to" for everything. Music brings me joy. It brings me peace. It brings me comfort. It brings me healing. It brings me freedom. It brings me to God. Praise and worship music is my battle armor. I can't do without it. It is like oxygen to me. I really enjoy it even when it is hard to worship!

I usually put my music on or find a radio station and let it just blast through the building. This is a regular occurrence in my house. The boys know if it's loud, don't bother Mom. She's in her secret place! Sometimes they join me, but most times they just study me or laugh. I know that it is shaping them, though, and that's all I want. I find them singing praise at quiet or unexpected moments. I just smile. God, You are so good!

I compile a list of songs that I really enjoy. They lift my spirits and take me to a place higher than my reality. I just move from one to the other. I even listen to sermons in between the songs and join those worship services. The boys sometimes go to church at times when I can't, and when they return, they run up the stairs to my room only to hear me shouting hallelujahs. They open the bedroom door, stare, smile, and back out slowly. Mom is having church!

This was one of those moments. One of those Sundays. I was missing a lot of church. My spirit was willing—actually, I desired to go—but my flesh was weak. This particular health battle lasted almost a year! My prayers seemed to go unanswered, and I was desperate for God to meet me. I put on the music and trampled the enemy. I was glad to be home alone. I stomped all around my room as best I could with a pic line in my arm and a nephrostomy tube out my back connected to a bag on my leg! How had I ended up here? What started out as one surgery was now onto the fourth. I had also had four major infections that were now life-threatening. We were making the emergency room our second home.

I was really tired of this journey. I was hurting physically, but my heart was hurting more. So I did the only thing I knew to do: I chose to fight the sadness with prayer and praise. I turned on some praise and worship music. I learned to practice worshipping God, no matter what the circumstances. Today I was going to create an atmosphere of worship.

God promises us peace that surpasses all understanding in Philippians 4:7, *"And the peace of God, which transcends all understanding, will guard your hearts and your minds in Christ Jesus"* (NIV). That promise follows Philippians 4:4, which instructs us, *"Rejoice in the Lord always. I will say it again: Rejoice!"* (NIV).

Since I believe the Word of God to be true, I had to first obey that instruction. That atmosphere of worship didn't remove all the tubes that were stuck in my body, but it once again carried me to Jesus, who carried me on that day and the days that followed. My situation didn't change at this moment in time, but being in a place of worship and thanksgiving changed my soul. I let the truth of who God is soothe my spirit. I felt His power. I was mindful of God's presence, so I wasn't going to allow my feelings to drive my actions. I sensed His presence as He comforted my weary soul. Gratitude shifted my gaze to see Jesus instead of my circumstance, and my heart found a place of joy to rest in for awhile.

I will praise You, O Lord my God, with all my heart, And I will glorify Your name forevermore (Psalm 86:12)

I found God again. He is good. He brought His joy.

Chapter Fourteen
THE BATTLE IS THE LORD'S

The room was filled with praises and prayer warriors who had gathered together on my behalf. I felt so loved and so strengthened. We sang familiar songs that encouraged me. We read Scriptures that kept my faith firm. There was power in the room, and power in our lives. I went to bed feeling certain that my miracle was on its way!

As we sat around the waiting room the next day, we were happy, laughing with the nurses and talking with strangers. We were filled with expectation: this was going to be my day! When my name was called, I kissed my husband, and we left each other in a state of peace. "I'll see you soon," I said, and smiled as he left to go have some breakfast with our pastor.

It was *really* soon—only about half an hour. That was sooner than any of us had expected—so soon that they weren't back to get me when I came out. I waited. I sang songs and recited Scriptures. By the time they did return for me, they found me with a big smile on my face. They couldn't wait to hear my news, and I couldn't wait to share it! They needed to hear what had happened from the beginning.

I'd lain on the table and heard the voices lower to a very faint whisper. The sedation hadn't knocked me out—I couldn't feel anything, but I could still hear their voices. I'm not sure that they were aware of that, and I couldn't tell them. I felt like I was in a dream.

My ears didn't want to hear what I was hearing, but they had no choice. The procedure didn't work. It wouldn't work. There was a blockage, and they still didn't know what was causing it. There would have to be another major surgery scheduled—the sixth one! As I heard the words, "We need to retube her and send her home. We can't do anything further right now," I wanted to sink into deep sadness.

My heart was in tension with my emotions. I knew God was greater than what was happening. My spirit said, "Fight with your spiritual weapons." I knew that if I didn't let my spirit win, I would go to a place I didn't want to be. So in my semiconscious state, I began to quote Scriptures. I am sure the practitioners just thought it was the anaesthetic having an effect on me. The peace I had entered the room with began to wash over me again.

When my husband and pastor came back for me, I was all smiles. They found me singing. They both told me I looked good. They wanted to know how everything had gone, so I told them. They were so surprised that I felt I had to comfort them. They were left without words.

On the operating table, I paraphrased Romans 8:31, declaring, "God is for me and not against me."

Though He slay me, yet will I hope in Him… (Job 13:15, NIV)

I was going to keep trusting God, and while I waited for the healing I chose to do what I always did. Pray. Praise. Cry. Read and receive the Word. Repeat. The nurses upstairs were surprised to see me so soon. They'd planned on seeing me later, and just for the recovery period. They'd hoped that this was going to be the last time they saw me. We all did. I told them they couldn't get rid of me so fast. We laughed again. I left them the way I had greeted them that morning—I cheered them up. I found God again that day. He brought me His peace that passes all understanding.

Chapter Fifteen

THE WAY TO A MAN'S HEART

They say the way to a man's heart is through his stomach. Well, my husband's heart had been getting fed for months, and so had his belly. My boys were just as happy. They are just like their dad—they enjoy food. During one season of life, we had the privilege of eating so many different types of meals we hadn't eaten before. The homemade dishes made with love were coming regularly, and my boys' palates were opening up to new tastes!

I love cooking. I love it more because my boys love to eat. They enjoy what I make for them—most of the time!

We enjoyed such flavourful soups, had different kinds of rice and noodles, tried roasted pork, had a delicious BBQ, and ate tasty roasted vegetables. My fridge and freezer were always full. My kitchen smelled like an Italian restaurant when my good friend came to show us how to make foccacia! It was my boys' new favourite for awhile. God was opening our eyes and stomachs to the truth of us being blessed. There is nothing like a meal to bring people together! The sharing of time, conversation, effort and love that comes from gathering around food brings joy to me.

It was an exciting time. We were on a food frenzy! We were living our own cooking channel and food truck experience! I couldn't ask for more. The blessings were flowing with great ease. God had overwhelmed my heart and home with His sweet aroma through the fragrance of food. My cup ran over, and we were never in want. At just the right time the doorbell always rang, and there was someone at my door or a gift certificate in my mailbox to provide a meal. We sometimes had too much! God gave in abundance, and life was good. Well, maybe not all of it!

As much as I enjoyed (and enjoy) cooking, none of the meals were being prepared by me. They were being prepared for me. I was in shock at how God took care of every detail for my family, not just by all the cooking my own extended family did, but my colleagues and church family, too. I shouldn't have been surprised, but I was. This was one area of our lives in this journey I never had to think about. God really did provide our daily bread. God really did show Himself through meeting the practical need of having meals. This happened almost daily for over two years!

Sometimes in life there is plenty to thank God for and at the same time plenty of lack. At this time in our lives, we lived in two seasons simultaneously! We had so much to thank God for taking us through. Yet we were in such need. God met us at both places.

> Gratitude unlocks the fullness of life. It turns what we have into enough and more. It turns denial into acceptance, chaos to order, confusion to clarity. It can turn a meal into a feast, a house into a home, a stranger into a friend. (Melody Beattie[2])

"At least I don't have cancer," I'd heard myself say many times. But those words couldn't be said anymore. They couldn't. After two weeks of repeated testing it was confirmed. The doctor's 98% certainty that I had cancer was now 100% confirmed. Before,

I used to say that sentence because I wanted to emphasize that someone else's situation was worse than mine. I'd repeated that phrase because two times in the previous year and another time in my past I had come face to face with this possibility. Each time, God had spared me from that fact becoming my reality.

In fact, as you have read, I had just gone through a year in which I went under the knife with anaesthetic six times! The hospital staff on different floors got to know me very well. The poor nurse at admitting and surgery was so sorry to see me every time I came in. I was becoming a real fixture at the ambulatory care and emergency ward. I had just completed what I thought would be my last surgery only six months prior. I was now on my healing journey! The nurses and doctors celebrated our time together coming to an end. They genuinely loved seeing me weekly, but genuinely didn't want to see me anymore.

I kept saying that phrase because I was finding something to be thankful about. Since the cancer scare had come up more than once and had always been a false alarm, although I was experiencing a year that I wouldn't wish even on my worst enemy, I felt that there was going to be an end and I would finally be healed. I could get through this.

While this was happening, I had two friends experiencing a battle with cancer. I saw the changes that were happening to their bodies and their self-image. I saw how sick and frail they became. For one friend, the battle didn't have an end date in the foreseeable future. For the other, although there was an end in sight, each day presented a very difficult road.

Many wondered how I was going from one surgery to another, while I wondered what I could do to help my two friends. My journey wasn't easy; however, I felt blessed that I didn't have to use major poison to kill poison while not knowing what that would mean for my body, in the present or the future. I felt my journey still left me with some sense of control. I couldn't control what was happening *to* my body, but I still had some control in what I could do *with* my body.

I will spare you most of the graphic details, but just to give you an idea of what was happening, I'd originally had surgery to remove growths in my ovaries and repair tubes that had grafted to my hip bones. A few months after that, I suddenly found myself haemorrhaging. This happened for three months without stopping. I went in for the major surgery of the hysterectomy. What followed? Five more months with five more surgeries; the nephrostomy tube, infections, and pic line I mentioned earlier; and finally a reconstructive reimplantation surgery! Then six months after my last surgery came the diagnosis of cancer.

And worship continued. Pray. Praise. Cry. Read and receive the Word. Repeat. That Christmas season, I was once again having surgery on December 23rd. Once again, though, God's present was being at home to celebrate with my family on December 25th. I even went to church on Christmas Eve! Worship. Celebrate. Repeat!

In my distress I called upon the Lord,
And cried out to my God… (Psalm 18:6)

Heal me, O Lord, and I shall be healed;
Save me, and I shall be saved,
For You are my praise… (Jeremiah 17:14)

I chose to face this, surrendering to God and continuing in the battle pattern I had set for myself. The Lord had taken me through the last year, and He was going to take me through this one. I was going to continue to be intentional about committing myself to prayer and praise. Worshipping God was still going to be first in my life. Life was so uncertain, but God was certain. He was faithful.

I have learned the same lesson many times. Life changes. God remains the same. When I focus on God and let His truth nourish my heart, my faith and trust in Him grow, so this was just another lesson in trust.

> Life changes. God remains the same.

My doctor called me personally. I remember that phone call well. I remember where I was standing and what the weather was like. The sun was out, although it was cold and windy. There were moments when I felt drops of rain. That was how I felt. I felt the warmth of God's presence and fought off the cold feelings of despair that wanted to grip my attention. Instead, I looked up at the sky and laughed. I felt like I was literally laughing at the enemy. I declared "Satan, you are going to lose again. The Lord took me through the last battle, and I will come out of this one!" My mind quickly focussed on the truth that God had been trustworthy in the not-so-distant past, and I could trust Him to be faithful now and in my future. I let tears form. Some fell, but I wasn't going to walk in the rain without remaining in the light of God.

I'm not going to lie and say that the cancer journey was an easy one, but although it was hard, it wasn't as horrific as it could have been. Two weeks after my surgery, the incision burst open and was infected. The nurse came every day for eight weeks and packed the wound with gauze until it closed. But even in that time, I felt that God led me to the right help, choices and support. The nurses were amazing. They became new friends. It would take another book to discuss everything that happened on my cancer journey—maybe I will write it one day, but for now I can tell you that I continued to pray and praise and cry through the good and bad times.

God was with me when I cut my hair to get ready for the possibility of losing it. I'd had long hair all my life. It was my pride and joy. I felt beautiful with my hair. I loved my hair! If I was going to lose my hair, then I was going to be in control of how that happened. I learned that I don't look too bad with shorter hair!

My co-workers were so surprised when I walked through the door of the school. For over nineteen years, they had only seen me with very long hair. This was a new look, and it went over well. I had chosen to cut twelve inches off to prepare for what treatment would most likely do to me. I'd had no intention of taking any treatment and had sought out three different specialists in the naturopathic field. I'd already had the surgery and was taking the right natural health steps to make me stronger. I also prayed and sought counsel from trusted friends and family. But all three gave the same advice: take traditional treatment along with naturopathic therapy. So what do you do when you have prayed and the signs are so undeniable that you know it must be God speaking? What do you do when God gives you an answer you don't want to hear? You pray. You praise. You cry. You read and receive the Word. You obey!

I continued with naturopathic oncology support, and also completed traditional chemo and radiation. I found God again. He is good. He did give an answer, though not the one I'd wanted. He answered with clarity, and when I accepted His leading, He gave a peace that passed understanding.

Chapter Sixteen
CELEBRATE GOOD TIMES

It was cold and wet and windy. Visibility on the roads was uncertain at times. But I had laser vision. I took comfort in knowing Che was a great driver and was right by my side. We had the awesome privilege of witnessing the daughter of my colleague (who was also a dear friend) marrying the love of her life. I had the honour of performing the wedding ceremony. I was looking forward to this. I was so thankful to God that I could do this. I had strength. The joy of the Lord was truly my strength.

Inside the venue, the chatter of the guests and the expectation of what was to come filled the room with sunshine and warmth. The weather outside was a distant memory. There was much to celebrate, and the music and aroma of delicious food that filled the air encouraged people to join the celebrations. I am sure that wasn't too hard for most! Once inside, the fesitivites drew you into a new and even better atmosphere. It was truly a beautiful evening.

Che stayed close in proximity to me with his eyes and heart. He knew I needed this evening. This was another strong example of God's strength being made perfect in me. There was no other way to explain how I was standing—let alone milling about and making conversation while about to perform a wedding ceremony!

We found my friend. She looked at me, joyous to be sharing this moment, but searching me with her eyes. She didn't know what she was looking for, but she could tell that something wasn't right. She hadn't seen my new hair! I hadn't told her how my week had been, or how this particular day had unfolded. I didn't want to worry her. I wanted to keep my commitment. I was so thankful that God had blessed me so I could bless them!

We couldn't stay once the ceremony was over. I had no choice but to tell her why—my hairstyle gave it away, but my countenance wouldn't allow her attention to stray longer than a minute from that momentous evening ahead. Her focus was to be on her daughter.

I did what I came to do, knowing that Che was praying me through it. Seeing his gaze kept assuring me that God had brought me this far, and I was having victory in this moment. The entire family and guests really enjoyed the ceremony. None but my friend knew until some time later what state I had been in. It was a truly beautiful evening. The Lord was radiating through me as I looked to Him, and I thank Him that there was no shame. I really don't know how God did it.

I look back now and know what I did was crazy—but I'd known that as soon as we got back in the car! I spent the rest of the weekend more sick than I'd anticipated, but I would make the same choice again. Life is no fun without crazy. I am crazily in love with God. I am crazily stubborn to keep believing God for the hard things. I am crazily committed to being used by God to bless others, even when the odds are against me. I look back and thank God for allowing me to be crazy. I have a crazy memory that puts a smile on my face, and they have a beautiful memory that will be forever in their hearts! God was faithful to me again in yet another difficult time. I look back and think to myself, enemy, you lost again! I did what God wanted me to do to bless others. I was more than a conqueror. Thanks be to God, Who gave me victory again!

I didn't get a chance to even say goodbye to most. We had to move quickly! By the time we got to the car, it came strong. Che really wanted to get me home. I was thankful that God had put us alone together, as we went back to experiencing our reality. I didn't ruin anyone's special day. On the ride home, I moaned and groaned, but was still very grateful. I wasn't feeling as bad as I had all day!

The truth was that God had given strength for the week and day—in times and ways I needed in spite of my present reality. I had just completed my first chemo treatment that Monday. The wedding was the following Friday. The first couple days had been good. I fought nausea, but it was a little better than my pregnancies, so I fought well. And then everything changed.

That Thursday night and all of Friday until an hour before I got ready to go to the wedding, I begged God to help and change my circumstances. I prayed and cried. I called and texted others to request their prayers. This was hard. I spent most of my time being carried to and from the washroom, too sick to describe. I was in and out of consciousness, blacking out after every episode of vomiting. I was amazed that could even happen, considering I'd barely eaten! I had never experienced such weakness, or at least in those moments it felt that way. "God, where are You? You have to help me. I can't let them down. There is no wedding without me." All these thoughts filled the short moments when I was conscious enough.

Che kept telling me there was no way I could do it, and I needed to think of my options. I kept telling him there was no way I wasn't doing it and that was my only option! Only God. It could only be Him. I found God to be good again. He strengthened and used me to be a blessing.

Chapter Seventeen
TWO IS BETTER THAN ONE

My friend had been on this journey a few years before I started mine. She was there to meet me on my road, and we walked it together. She was a real pillar of strength and encouragement for me. What a prayer warrior! I looked forward to our weekly prayer times together. They were so refreshing. We believed God would bring us miracles. In fact, this friend was the one who a year earlier had arranged a prayer meeting for me before one of my surgeries, even though she was battling health problems herself. We kept each other strong during this fight. I always looked forward to communicating with her, and us bringing each other to God together.

One day she left. It was a sudden move and it took me by surprise, yet it shouldn't have! She was a real blessing to me, and I wasn't taking this move well. She was moving far away, and it would be a long time before I would see her again.

I watched her go. It was something I'd never thought I would witness. I was there as a pastor, yet she was my friend. I don't think I held it together. I came home numb—a mess. I had just watched my friend die. I'd lost my friend! Pray. Praise. Cry. Read and receive the Word. Repeat.

I gave a tribute and spoke at her farewell celebration. It was a privilege to speak about her and to invite others to follow her example of faith. I didn't know how I was going to do it, though. I cried for many days after. I argued with God every day as well. The morning I prepared my speech, I thought I would never be able to deliver it, but God gave me such power and strength. The words just flowed freely from my mouth. With boldness and conviction, I spoke about her strong belief that God is a miracle-working God. Through her journey, He had worked many miracles. I could not forget that, and I couldn't let others forget that either. I recited the words from two great songs, one by Kutless[3] and the other by Mercy Me[4]—both called "Even If." Both songs allude to trusting God in spite of what may happen in life.

I couldn't believe that I was sharing about faith—yes, hers in this moment, but mine as well, because during this time, I was also questioning God. How could He let this happen? Why didn't He heal her when she had no doubt in her mind that He would? We both expected Him to, and that's why her move had been so sudden. I knew she was deteriorating, but we hadn't even entertained the possibility that it would end this way. We knew that even in the most desperate of times, God is greater. Even that last day in the hospital, and in those last moments, I believed that God was going to let her live or raise her from the dead.

Why did she die, and why was I left living? How could I speak of God working miracles when my friend lay breathless and lifeless before me? Even the moment before I got up to give my tribute, these questions and more raced through my thoughts. How was I going to speak of faith in God when I felt I had none? Then the words just left my mouth. God was speaking through me in that moment to bring comfort to others, but speaking to me in His gentle voice at the same time, reminding me that what I believed about Him hadn't changed. God still knew best, and even if I didn't get the answer I wanted, it didn't change who He was and is! I was to trust and believe, but I was not responsible for any outcome. In that moment, my heart perspective was changed. I hadn't lost my friend. She'd just moved to a better home. I would see her again. I can't wait to see her again! Through my tears, I found God to be the friend that sticks closer than a brother. I found Him, whispering in my ears that He had her, and He has me, too.

Chapter Eighteen
TO BE CONTINUED

For I am convinced that neither death nor life, neither angels or demons, neither the present nor the future, nor any powers, neither height nor depth, nor anything else in all creation, will be able to separate us from the love of God that is in Christ Jesus our Lord. (Romans 8:38–39, NIV)

There have been many days when I've questioned God's choices for me these last few years. I'm still not sure why I've had to go through so many struggles, but I know that God loves me and has a purpose—even if I can't see it. He has used me in these difficulties, and for that I am thankful. The nurses that came to do home care for me allowed me to pray with them, and one also ended up going back to church. At school, I was able to testify to God's strength being what carried me through. I still taught on the days when my body was strong enough. I learned how to wrap head scarves and became a more fashionable woman. I enjoyed ministry on the worship team on Easter and Mother's Day during chemo treatment. I preached a week after the cancer surgery. I had great visits from friends and family that made me laugh and feel loved. I started writing this book. God was still giving me reasons to have a heart of gratitude!

Surgery after surgery brought more complications. Whenever I thought things couldn't get worse, they would. I did have moments of sitting in the bathtub in a lot of pain, crying and wondering how long this was going to last. Then cancer came. I had moments when I'd be standing in the shower, wanting the water to bring comfort, but it would only add more pain as each drop stung my body. I experienced great sadness in those moments, as I longed for my former life.

I stood in quietness and disbelief before God many times, with no choice but to witness and accept the war my body was waging on itself. My hair was dry and brittle like straw, and would fall out in clumps. This happened right after the first treatment. Many times my emotional, spiritual and physical energy was so drained, I felt I had doubled my age in just a few short months. I had mouth sores. I had nausea. I lost my sense of taste. I spent too many days in the hospital, fighting off infection or having another surgery or with no immune system to fight off disease. There were hard days that lasted years! Yet I was amazed by how God made the time go by fast when gratitude filled my heart and mind.

I also had moments of sitting in the bathtub, allowing the music on the phone to wash over my spirit and soothe my emotional and spiritual pain. The words were just what I needed every time. The alone time was also what I needed. My family gave me that gift while they carried on with life as usual. I wanted them to. I didn't want what I was going through to have an adverse effect on them, and I can only say that God did it again. The boys still excelled in school. They continued with their sports and music. They had great friends whose parents kept them for play dates. They were still having the time of their lives, and God protected their spirits so that they could continue with life. I lived vicariously through my boys. I was so proud of them. I had three "men" who remained strong, taking care of each other, our home and me. I would wait with anticipation to hear how their days at school went or how a sporting event had turned out.

"I scored a hat trick!"

"I gave an amazing assist!"

I would get the play-by-play. I would relive the games in my imagination, and we would celebrate how proud I was of them.

I learned their love languages. One son would sit by my bed and do his homework. He would cuddle up to me and just needed us to be touching while he watched YouTube videos on the laptop. My other son would just peek his head in and need to hear an affirming word from me. He rarely came close. But I watched him carefully. He grew in independence. He wanted to show me he was strong and could take care of himself. He loved to receive little gifts from me if I picked something up from the hospital or treatment appointments. They were all so strong. They grew up so fast before I could blink. They served me. They put a bell by my bed that I could ring if I needed them to come and help. They checked on me to ask if I'd walked or gone to the bathroom or eaten. They took me for walks down the stairs, around the kitchen, or just down the driveway. They would hold my hand tightly and cheer me on.

My husband was a warrior. He stayed so strong. He was *Driving Miss Daisy, Mr. Mom, Daddy Day Care* and *Superman* all in one. My heart is filled with gratitude and my eyes still well with tears when I think about it. I'm not sure who was more tired. He worked so hard inside and outside our home. He made sure everything worked like a well-oiled machine. I checked in many times and asked how he was doing. He never complained. I prayed. I praised. I cried. I read and received the Word. Repeat. I never wanted them to see me sick or to have to go through these last three years. I never wanted to miss so much of their lives. I felt both guilty and grateful. They truly amazed me. There is no doubt in my mind that I am loved.

I knew the church was praying, and this was how my husband and boys were well-taken care of. I thank God that He allowed me to still pray daily with my prayer partners. I wasn't going to give that up! He gave me moments of grace to pray for them, and them for me. I look back on the phone messages I saved and see the texts sent to people. I made a choice to be thankful for what was going well, and to share that with others so I could remain in a positive space. Others sent positive, uplifting messages to me. This cycle carried me. Pray. Praise. Cry. Read and receive the Word. Repeat.

This didn't just happen by itself—it involved so many others. When I didn't feel I could make it through another day, I just sent out messages telling my friends that I needed to be carried, and I was! At other times, God sent messages to me when I least expected it. A card with just the right words would come in the mail. A phone call from a friend with a word of knowledge or encouragement would come at just the right time in the day. A spoken word from my boys, telling me that I was brave and beautiful, even when I was bald! God was very detailed in ministering to me.

Everyone always tells me that I am an inspiration. I didn't set out to be. Many can't figure out how I remain so positive—I just know that my hope is in the Lord, and I want others to see Him through me in life's entire journey. Perspective is key. My heart has to remain filled with gratitude and thankfulness, so that I can always see that I have enough. This is one key in my ability to weather the storms. They will come, and I want to remain prepared at all times. Encouraging others encourages me. Being with people while doing what I love fuels me. I might have been sick many times, but there was still

> When bad surrounds you, you have to look for the good. Good is there because God is there, and He is good!

a lot I could do because God gave me strength. So I did what I could: I lived life. I made the best with what I had. Truly I was strong in the Lord and the power of His might. When bad surrounds you, you have to look for the good. Good is there because God is there, and He is good!

The answers to the difficult seasons in life are rarely obvious, but the answer for our help is God. He cares, and is in every detail. I must make the choice to find Him. I am too positive to stay in doubt, too optimistic to let fear grow, and have too much determination to let defeat take a position in my life. I don't travel alone. With God, I will move forward.

Living by faith means taking one step at a time, and sometimes standing still in between each step to pray, praise, and cry. In the stillness, there is strength.

Truly my soul silently waits for God… (Psalm 62:1)

Be still, and know that I am God… (Psalm 46:10)

It is here, in this practice, that I have found peace for my travels along the road God laid out for me. My peace is more important than trying to understand why life unfolds the way it does. I have had to "Let go and let God" many times. I invite God to be my constant partner, and He accepts the invitation.

God uses hard times and tragedy to shape us, but they must not define us. God has already done that!

We are blessed and highly favoured.

We are more than conquerors.

We are not alone.

We are loved.

We are His.

I heard someone say that we grow far more through pain than through pleasure. I look back and celebrate how far I've come! I have done so with God at my side. I've continually found God through my journey because I've made it a practice to talk with Him, to worship His Name, and to celebrate His power at work in my life.

God started me on a journey of prayer and praise when I was a little girl. I am still on that journey. Prayer and praise have kept me through the dark clouds, up the steep mountains, and down into the valley, and they've kept me fed and quenched in the places of drought.

God's arms held me when I was weak. His eyes looked at me through the darkness, and His presence brought light. He smiled on me with reassurance. He held me in His heart, and loved me through it all. I don't know what lies ahead, but I do know that He goes with me. I don't understand why there have been so many clouds in my skies, but I know that God is the one lifting me above the clouds and shining His light beneath them.

Jesus is the One I will follow. He is the One Who will guide me each day. He is the One I can share my whole heart with in prayer and praise. He is the One for me to listen to, and the One who hears me. He is the One who brings me reassurance through His Word and promises. I know that even if I think God is hiding, I will find him at the next turn in my journey, waiting to travel with me. He isn't finished with me yet. The journey continues.

BIO

Shireen Spencer is a gifted preacher and motivational speaker who loves to share her story of what God has done through her struggles to encourage and bring healing to others suffering the same challenges and heartaches. She is a pastor, an associate with Family Life Canada, an elementary school teacher, and a Mary Kay business owner. She is also a fully trained, equipped, and licensed officiant and life celebration professional. She's been described as friendly, gregarious, and passionate about bringing out the best in people. She is married to the love of her life, Che Spencer, and together they have two wonderful boys. They currently reside in the Greater Toronto Area.

REFERENCES

[1] Spencer, Shireen. "My Life is a Song."

[2] Beattie, Melody. (2017, December 31). "Gratitude." Retrieved from http://melodybeattie.com/gratitude-2/

[3] Kutless. (2012). "Even If." On Believer. BEC Recordings.

[4] MercyMe. (2017). "Even If." On Lifer. Fair Trade Services/Sony Music.